Conflicted Hearts

A daughter's quest for solace from emotional guilt

D.G. Kaye

ISBN: 978-0-9920974-2-4

Trade Paperback Release: December 2013

Disclaimer

Conflicted Hearts is a work of nonfiction. It has been written using the author's best recollection of events that took place in her life, which are conveyed to the best of her knowledge. In order to maintain the anonymity of those mentioned, the author has changed the names of individuals and places, as well as some identifying characteristics and details, such as physical descriptions, occupations, and places of residence.

Contents

Dedication

To my best friends, Zan and Bri, for always being there for me with an emotional rescue. I love you both.

Acknowledgments

I'd like to thank my siblings: my two brothers, Rory and Robby, for allowing me to write about our lives, and my sister, Melanie, for cheering me on for years to, "Write the book already!" I also thank my husband, Gordon, for his continuous support while I wrote this book and for his many sacrifices and dinners along the way.

Special thanks to my reader/friend Antonella Hartman and my colleague, author James Thorn (http://JThorn.net), for his support and advice during the making of this book.

Additional thanks to:
Editors: Talia Leduc and Katy Sozaeva
Cover Design and Book Design: jdsmith-design.com

Preface

As far back as I can remember, I liked to write about my feelings. I wanted a voice, but when I was small, children were supposed to be seen and not heard. That was a phrase I remember being told many times as a child. I did not speak out, but I did keep notes on the events that unfolded throughout my childhood, recording them in a mental journal over the years until I grew older, when I thought I would perhaps consider writing about them . . . someday.

Writing this book has been a cathartic cleansing of my soul, which had become a crowded closet, filled with the clutter of unresolved feelings that were long overdue for a good purging. I began to piece together the fragments of my past, which had left heavy footprints in my thoughts as I navigated through life and which, I am quite sure, helped form my personality along the way. I wanted to comprehend the complexities of my parents and their upbringings because, surely, their personalities had also been formed by their pasts.

I truly believe that we are all the sum of our experiences.

As I grew older, I discovered answers to the questions that had plagued me as a child and subsequently influenced the choices I made. My inner turmoil stemmed from the unease I had felt in my mother's presence, her volatile and narcissistic temperament having instilled a constant nervousness and insecurity within me, while my ongoing sympathy was rooted in my father's sadness, as he had allowed himself to be repeatedly subjected to my mother's antics while totally blinded by her physical beauty.

I have also discovered that we only think we can bury our pasts—because the past has a strange way of lingering. Mother-guilt never goes away, no matter how far we physically distance ourselves from it. As much as I try to do the right things in life, I have certainly made my share of mistakes. However, I always try to learn something from them. My mistakes have become my teachers. For me there is a reason for every action and, through the years, I have learned to take these reasons with a dose of positivity.

Through writing this book, I have realized my compassion and learned forgiveness, though I do not believe anyone should have to remain in a situation with no resolution simply because she has forgiven.

Introduction

By nature, a child begins life innocent, not questioning whether hers is a normal childhood because she has only her parents to trust that it is. As children are initially conditioned by a familiar home environment, having yet to be exposed to outside influences, most children never question whether their upbringings would be considered normal. However, some kids have an inherently good grasp on which situations are not conducive to a normal childhood, and once these children are set out into the world, outside teachings and influences begin to awaken their curiosity. Only then may these children begin to question the state of their own homes.

There are children who cruise through life indifferent to its intricacies, as life is much too complicated for a young child to comprehend. In some cases, these children grow up on autopilot, going through the motions. They may never question the normalcy of their lives. In other cases, the doubts may linger—perhaps until these children grow older—and only then might they want to delve back in time to satisfy the years of unasked questions. If a child can find answers to the mysteries in her mind and then find solace in those answers, there is hope that she may understand her past and begin to repair the inner damages that are still raw and naked to her loved ones' eyes.

I was raised in silent pain. Although I was no authority

on childrearing, I knew in my soul at a very young age that I hadn't been given all the tools necessary for a happy, encouraging childhood. When I say this, I don't refer to food, clothes, or toys, as those things were thankfully not lacking in our home. Instead, I mean that I grew up emotionally unfulfilled, always afraid of the fallout from my parents' relationship, harboring a constant sadness. My mother was barely ever home, and when she was, I was very careful not to speak my feelings and I was afraid to ask any questions that would make her temper flare. My stomach would churn in anticipation of her response, always dependent on her mood for the day.

As for my sadness, I always worried about my father—it was as though our roles had been reversed and I was forced to be a parent to him. My mother had evicted him so many times throughout my childhood that I often felt as though I were living on a seesaw, never knowing from one day to the next if my daddy would be coming home. I questioned everything throughout my childhood, and I was constantly disappointed when there were no answers. As time progressed, I knew that I had to figure out the answers for myself.

When I was a very little girl, I had an uncanny sixth sense for the emotions of others, an almost adult awareness of my environment. Back then, I liked to think of it as some sort of inner survival instinct. Growing up in an emotionally unstable environment, I felt as though it was my job to pay close attention to the happenings in my household, particularly those involving my parents. I believed that paying attention would enable me to stay one step ahead of things. Of course, I didn't always know what went on behind closed doors, but much was said around us children under the assumption that we weren't listening, being seen but not heard, oblivious as all children are thought to be.

Well, I was listening.

Vacancy

When I think of my mother, Helen of Troy always comes to mind: the face that launched a thousand ships—and the Trojan horse.

When I was a small child, before I realized how broken my home was, I was enamored by my mother's physical beauty. It seemed anyone who crossed her path was smitten by her. Even through the emotional neglect I endured as a child and into my teen years, I thought I wanted to be just like her. Her physical beauty commanded attention, and perhaps her minimal presence in my life had become the very reason I adored her.

I had yet to fully understand the power of her manipulation. Though I had witnessed my mother doling out humiliation to my father, I realized little beyond a dim awareness of the inner sadness I carried for him. I grew up with no understanding of all the little secrets in our household, unaware that the seeming adoration I held for my mother would become the very thing I learned to resent her for as I grew older.

Throughout my childhood and teen years, my mother was vacant. I have no recollection of spending any time, let alone quality time, with my mother while growing up. Even when she wasn't gallivanting out of town with friends, she was never home. After my parents separated, we had babysitters until I reached the age of twelve, when I became the babysitter. If my mother went out of town, she would arrange for a family friend to stay with us during her absence. If we were really lucky, our Aunty Sherry, my mother's sister, would stay with us. Those were the best times.

Aunty Sherry didn't get married until later in life, and being single allowed her to spend lots of time with us. She gave us so much love, and we laughed all the time with her. She even drove us to school and picked us up. We loved it when she took us to the movies, and she would take us to Mighty Midget, our local variety store, and let us pick out candies. When she stayed over, my siblings and I would huddle together on the couch and watch movies together with her. I cherished the time we spent with Aunty Sherry.

The weekends followed a pattern. On Friday night, my dad would take us to our paternal grandparents' house, where we spent every weekend from the time I was a toddler to the age of fourteen. This wasn't a choice; it was life as we knew it. My dad would stay for dinner and come back again on Saturday afternoon for lunch and a visit with us, and he would return midmorning on Sunday to take us back home. This little setup worked out quite well for my mother, who had every weekend off from her children despite hardly ever being home during the week. To this day, I can't get over how my mother got away with all of it. It wasn't that she worked or had a business, just that she loved to be anywhere but home. Home was merely a place where she could do her hair and makeup and change her clothes.

Sadly, I have no memories of my mother doing any "mommy things" with me. She wasn't there to help with my homework, to make me breakfast or lunch, and she was rarely home to make dinner. She wasn't there to watch TV with me, to take me shopping, or even to drive me or pick me up from school. When I was six, I used to take myself and my younger brother Rory on the fifteen-minute walk to kindergarten and then pick him up after school. When I would leave for school in the mornings, my mother was always sleeping, her car parked in the driveway. This pattern carried on through the births of my other three siblings. By the age of eleven, I had earned a whole host of other responsibilities. I made the beds, straightened up the house, cooked dinners, and learned a lot about laundry. Within another year, I had gained the pleasure of becoming a babysitter, as well.

*

Throughout my childhood, my parents split up more than half a dozen times. This usually meant my mother throwing my father out for indiscernible personal reasons. Occasionally, it meant my dad leaving on his own because he could no longer tolerate her.

My father was a meek man. His once blond hair had become sandy brown over the passing years, and he had tired of his widow's peak and changed his hairstyle to a comb-over. He radiated innocence, his good nature shining through. He was the kind of guy one couldn't help but like. He didn't have a lot to say, and he didn't have the heart to discipline harshly. He never raised his voice or his hand to any one of his children. Daddy was a hard worker in the family business, a fish company that had originally been opened as a fish market by his father back in the early 1930s. My dad and his only brother worked the business with my grandfather for many years until family politics intervened and changed the dynamic of the business.

My grandmother was born in a small town, her parents having migrated from Russia, whereas my grandfather was himself born in Russia. They were religious, hard-working people, quiet and devoid of outstanding personalities. It was evident that my grandmother wore the pants in their household, and my grandfather happily doted on her. They were simple folk who worked hard for their money and spent their whole lives watching their pennies and being devout Orthodox Jews. My father always seemed to have an inner fear of his parents and never dared argue with anything they said. However, I believe that deep down he rebelled against his parents' beliefs, and I know he had never intended to be a religious man.

Knowing my grandparents as I did, I knew that my father marrying my mother went against everything they believed in. First of all, my bastardly conception was frowned upon by my grandparents, and second, my grandparents never really accepted my mother because the Jewish religion is passed down the maternal line. Though my mother's father was Jewish, also born in Russia, her mother was of Scottish descent. To this day, my mother stands by her "story" that her mother converted to Judaism, though I have it on good authority that this was not so.

Nonetheless, even if she had converted, she was still a product of her own mother, and that just wasn't accepted by Orthodox Jewish standards. I didn't know whether these were the only reasons my grandparents didn't care for my mother; perhaps they saw something more that they didn't like. They never verbalized their dislike, though I figured it out myself through tidbits of comments my grandmother used to mutter under her breath, and I later confirmed this with my father.

My mother was an exquisitely beautiful woman. Nobody could pass her without turning to look twice. Her raven-black hair and her cat-like green eyes, accompanied by her perfect nose and high cheekbones, seemed to attract attention wherever she went. My mother looked regal. Her beautiful, flawless complexion remained lineless until well into her sixties. In actuality, she resembled Elizabeth Taylor, except her eyes were green instead of violet. Later in life, she became a redhead, and many people mistook her for Ann Margaret. She knew her beauty and reveled in it.

My mother came from a poor family. My maternal grandfather was a chicken farmer, a Russian Jewish immigrant. He married the love of his life, my grandmother, a Canadian-born Protestant who was known as a strikingly beautiful girl herself. In fact, my grandmother was a runner-up for the very first Miss Toronto Pageant in 1926. I never knew her; sadly, she died young after a car accident gave her a stroke. This left my mother, the youngest of six children at the age of fourteen, to muddle through life for herself. I was never told much of her past, only that my mother and her siblings all worked hard to get by and that my grandmother was a very strong, brazen woman who stood up to anyone who crossed her. Like my own mother, my maternal grandmother loved life and partying—and she possessed a fiery temper.

Childhood and Religion

As a child, I spent every weekend at my paternal grand-parents' home. This was by no means a fun or desirable event, but actually a plan devised by my mother, a great idea that would allow her to share the kids with the grandparents so she could have her freedom.

My grandparents were Orthodox Jews, though my family was not. I used the terrible term "going to jail" to refer to these mandatory weekends at their home. Perhaps this was a bit extreme, but it was exactly how I felt. For a child who went to school all week and who looked after her siblings starting at age twelve, the weekend should have been something to look forward to. However, the fact was that my grandparents were strict abiders of their faith, adhering to the laws of the Sabbath from sundown on Friday to sundown on Saturday. This meant that while in their home, we abided by those laws, as well.

We weren't allowed to watch TV or even listen to the radio. Nothing electrical was to be used, though the stove often remained on "simmer" during the Sabbath. I remember that this struck me as hypocritical: You couldn't turn the stove on, but if it had been turned on prior to the Sabbath, it would remain on and you could use it? This same rule applied when leaving certain lights on. I was such a precocious little girl, and I remember asking my grandfather—as I was still quite young but very curious—why we couldn't just do the same with the television. I thought this was brilliant. They left other things on, so why not the TV?

Well, that question didn't go over so well, and as with many questions I posed back then, I never received a real answer. My grandfather chuckled and shook his head at my gumption before responding, "You think you're such a clever little girl!" I suppose I should be thankful that there wasn't the same technology then that there is today, such as computers and video games, because I surely would have found it harder to endure those weekends if that were the case. As it was, there were four of us: me, my two brothers, and my baby sister. Using our creative imaginations, we made up games, built forts, played hockey cards, rolled marbles, and worked with whatever else tweaked our imaginations.

My grandparents weren't particularly warm, loving people. There were never any physical shows of emotion or even an, "I love you," and I was never on the receiving end of any sentiment they did happen to display. It took me many years, until I was well into my teens, having paid attention and analyzed the pieces of dialog I had gathered through the years, to figure out why they were so cold to me: I was the reason my father had married my mother, so their destructive relationship was my fault.

We continued spending weekends there until I was almost fourteen. It was then that I took a stand in protest. I spent so much time mentally rehearsing my statement in anticipation of the response I would receive from my mother, but I finally told her I didn't want to go to my grandparents' house anymore. What I didn't tell her was how ridiculous it was that we were being sent to stay with our grandparents, going stark raving mad with boredom, when these were the years we should have spent playing with friends on the weekend.

My mother responded, "Well, you can tell them, because they'll be very upset," but I didn't believe her. I had caught on to my mother by then. Of course it would be okay for me to tell them at that point, after so many years, because by then I was already taking care of my siblings, so we no longer needed looking after on weekends. I realized then that the change could no longer hamper my mother's lifestyle either way.

In Retrospect

Does time soften us, or is it the fear of being old and alone that makes us cling to those who are closest?

In those years, I missed music. It was always so quiet in my grandparents' house, save for when we were there, bringing signs of life. I don't remember hearing a single song over those weekends, and the old plastic transistor radio only played on Sunday mornings, tuned strictly to a news channel. Their life was so grey and uneventful that the time I spent there felt empty.

As far back as I can remember, music has been my escape. I loved music—and perhaps I even needed it, as it helped me shut out the discord of my family. In our home, there was always music playing, as though it was loved by each of us for our own comforting reasons. Music also filled the emptiness of our home, its words and melody having the uncanny ability to take us somewhere else. How could anyone live without music?

*

My paternal grandfather was a man of very few words. I don't remember him ever saying anything of interest, though I suppose that was because he never said much to me. He was cold and distant, and I was the black sheep in my family. I was the accident. After all, I had been cleverly used as the ploy to get my dad to marry my mother. Only after my grandmother had been dead for almost a decade, when my grandfather became old and fragile, did I begin to feel sorry for him. He was feeble and alone, and something in me had always known that if he had married someone other than my grandmother, he might have been able to show a softer side, a side that I had yearned to be loved by all my life.

I still went to visit him every few weeks, though my visits were short and dutiful. One day, as we were sitting on his worn leather couch in his grand family room, I was making small talk with him to fill in the long gaps of silence between words. I would indulge him on some tiny snippet of my life to keep the conversation flowing, as I always felt awkward around him, but this particular day was different. He looked at me and smiled, and then he said something I would never have thought him capable of saying. He said, "You know, you did turn out to be a good girl, after all."

I'm not absolutely sure, but I think this was his way of telling me something that took him a long time to figure out: that he did love me.

My grandmother was a very stern woman, and she had always looked old to me. I know she had worked hard with my grandfather in the fish store for many years before they became successful, and I suppose those labored years had taken a physical toll on her. Years of having her hands in cold water, cutting fish, had left her with bony and bent arthritic fingers. Long hours of standing in cold, damp freezers had left her with bulging varicose veins in her legs. She was a tough bird, with no warmth in her personality. Over all the weekends spent with her during my childhood, I never received any encouragement or praise, though I noticed that she doted on my siblings more than she ever did me.

As I got older, I began to understand through overheard comments that she didn't like my mother. When I figured out that my mother had become pregnant with me before marriage, my grandmother's resentment began to make sense. It wasn't until I was well into my teens that I realized why she had been so cold to me all my life: I had been the cause of my parents' union. However, that was no reason to emotionally neglect a child, and the realization just made me feel more contempt for my grandmother than I already had.

My grandmother was a devout woman with very old-fashioned morals. She could not accept the sin my mother had committed or the fact that my maternal grandmother hadn't really been Jewish—another unforgivable sin on a supposedly long list. My grandmother also abhorred my mother's lifestyle, though I could understand that much, because, as a mother, she only wanted the best for her son, my dad. Still, I could never understand why I, the child, was being punished for those sins.

My grandparents pretended to get along with my mother when we were small, but even a stranger could have detected the insincerity in their conversations. By the time I was eight my mother no longer partook in any holiday dinners at my grandparents' home, regardless of whether my parents were together or broken up. I suppose every ideal of the perfect Jewish family had been broken by my mother, and my grandparents couldn't accept it. I often wondered, as I got older, if just looking at me served as a constant reminder to my grandmother, a symbol of my mother's deceit.

I was in my mid-twenties when my grandmother died. I remember it well because it was such a strange and unsettling event for me. In the Jewish faith, people are buried the day after death, without being embalmed. The only exception to these religious laws is that if one dies on a Friday, there is no funeral until Sunday due to the Sabbath. The same rule applies if one dies on a holy day. Because my grandmother died on a holy day, the day before the Sabbath, she wasn't buried until three days later, and, for some reason I never understood, my grandfather kept her body in their home until the burial. She lay dead in her bed.

It was so macabre, and I was terrified of having to go to their house and see her dead body. When I arrived, my grandfather was in mourning, and my heart really did go out to him. They had nobody but one another and had been together for almost sixty years. The creepy part for me was when my grandfather asked me and my siblings to go into her room and say good-bye. At that point in my life, I had never even seen a dead body.

It was fall and still unseasonably warm, and when I went into her room, I couldn't help but avert my eyes and direct them toward the two huge industrial fans that stood erect at the foot of the bed. I recognized them immediately as being from the family fish plant. They had become a means to keep the room cool until the burial. We were ordered to kiss her on the cheek. The ritual itself was eerie enough, but it also reminded me of how uncomfortable I had always found it to kiss her while she was alive. Still, I didn't cry—I suppose all those years of being shown no affection had added up.

Her funeral was three days later. As I sat by my father's side in the limousine, en route to the ceremony, I saw the grief in my father's eyes and only then did I break out in tears. I knew in my heart that I wasn't crying for my grandmother but for my father, who sat pensively as he stared out the window in silence. I realized in that moment that no matter what resentments my father carried toward his mother; her passing had struck him deeply in his heart.

Stairs

Everything I learned about life outside school came to me through overheard adult conversations, television and, thankfully, my Aunty Sherry. On occasions that my mother was home and had company over, I loved to sit at the top of the stairway and listen in as my mother told her exciting stories. I found this little ritual to be quite informative, a way of learning about things to come.

Ever since I was a small girl, there had been unrest in our home. The disheartening question of whether my dad would be coming home from work haunted me each night, and worries consumed me throughout the school day. I kept thinking about home while I was in school, because I knew I was missing clues that could help me predict the mood of my parents' relationship each evening. I felt a constant need to know about things before they happened. Perhaps I felt I could prepare myself for things to come and thereby avoid the heart-wrenching shock I would feel each time I learned that my daddy wouldn't be coming home that night. At least, if I had witnessed their argument the previous night, I would know ahead of time that the odds of seeing my father around were slim.

I seemed to live my childhood in a state of continuous worry and anxiety. At school, it was hard concentrating on lessons while my dominant thoughts lay with my home life. It became my mission to pay close attention to all conversations at home so as to never miss these clues. It was as though I was playing a game of espionage. I would pretend to be otherwise engaged, perhaps while my mother was on the phone, and then I would turn on my radar. My best information came on those rare nights when my mother was hosting a friend, my aunt, or perhaps a poker game. She was never home just to spend time with us kids.

When we were sent to bed, my craft took shape. I assumed my position at the top of the stairs, allowing me a great hearing range. I would stay in that tiny corner for hours, careful not to make a sound. I couldn't let myself be discovered, as the fear alone of that happening was enough to set the butterflies in my stomach off in a tailspin. The hours would pass, and it was usually well after midnight before I would scamper into bed for fear of falling asleep in my corner. I may not have obtained all the information I was seeking, but I never forewent this ritual, and I was grateful to never have been caught throughout the years.

Summer Holidays

I remember crying myself to sleep so many nights. I was just a child who wanted her mother, and I tried to ignore the fear and unease I felt in her presence, because even that was better than the sadness I felt when she wasn't around.

My mother loved to gamble, plain and simple. She spent almost every day on her own at the racetrack, Monday through Saturday. Sometimes, as a Sunday family outing, she would take us kids along. That was our family entertainment. We would pull up to valet parking, and all the attendants knew her by name. She always had *her* table reserved in the dining room, where we got to order a fancy meal and watch the horses race through the window. During the times my parents were together, my dad would come along as well. People would come up to my mother and chat throughout the day, and no sooner had one man sat by her side, another would take his place. It was like a cult of horse owners, trainers, jockeys, and patrons. My mother seemed to know many people, as she had acquired some sort of status at the track.

When my dad came along, he would take us down to the paddocks, where we would watch the horses come out before a race. He would ask me to pick the horse I liked, and he would bet on a two-dollar ticket so I could have a horse to cheer for. It was exciting for me, as it was all I knew. After we finished eating lunch, my siblings and I would go down the escalator to the grandstand level, where the common folk, as I understood it, would stand around to watch the races. My favorite thing then was to collect the losing tickets that had been thrown away all over the dirty cement floors and examine them against race results to see if a winning ticket had accidentally been tossed away. By the time I was nine, I already had some knowledge of how to read the racing form.

For our annual summer vacations, we would go to the Fort Erie racetrack for two weeks every summer. Back in those days, the thoroughbred racing in Toronto ended sometime in July, and they would resume racing for the rest of the summer in Fort Erie. My mother, of course, went back and forth often throughout the summer run.

As children, my siblings and I looked forward to our summer vacation. It was fun, and there were always so many racetrack people around our motel. My Aunty Sherry also came to stay there for a few days when she wasn't working, and so did various other family members, friends, and acquaintances. During the rare times my parents weren't split up, my dad would come up on the weekends. Even though it was considered a family holiday, I still didn't get much quality time with my mother, as this was a very social time for her. My mother always booked two rooms, one for herself and one for us. Until I was about thirteen, my mother would bring a babysitter to stay with us, and we loved Fort Erie because we got to swim all day and play while Mom was at the track.

When the races were over, usually around five in the evening, my mother and all of her racetrack friends would come back to the motel, and the partying would begin. My mother's room seemed to be the hub of activity. Everyone would drink and laugh, and loud music played through open doors as people came and went between rooms. There were some horse owners, trainers, and jockeys who would stay at this motel, as well as lots of degenerate gamblers. We got to spend time in my mother's room and be part of the action for a little while every day, but then the babysitter would take us a block down the road to the usual restaurant for dinner. Afterward, we would go back to our room and watch TV before falling asleep. On the occasional night, Mom did join us for dinner.

It wasn't until my mid-teens that I began to piece together what had really been going on during those times back in Fort Erie. As a child, I had idolized my mother for all her beauty and the way men would swoon over her. I remember watching her dress in her makeup room, expertly applying her eyeliner with a winged tip, while I would catch my own anonymous reflection in her vanity mirror. I wanted so badly to look like her, so I could be beautiful too. I thought she had such a grand life, and I wanted to be just like her.

Eight

We are the products of our parents. How can they teach us what they didn't know?

Imagine feeling frustrated and powerless in a situation you're desperate to resolve. When you're a child, that angst multiplies immensely because you are only that—a child. You have no power to speak out about what you're feeling, and neither are you permitted to ask questions that might soothe your inner turmoil, because the cause of your dilemmas are adult matters that apparently shouldn't concern you.

I was eight, riding with my father in the car one Sunday afternoon. I looked forward to days like this because we were going downtown for breakfast at one of our favorite greasy spoons. This had become a regular jaunt for us most Sundays when my parents were separated, and I loved to eat my runny fried eggs with toast and hash browns, spending time with my father while taking in the goings-on in the busy little diner. This particular place was usually full of racetrack rounders, small-time gamblers, and bookmakers.

My dad was not a gambler, but he had frequented that diner for some time, having grown up not far from there. Through the years, the food had remained the same, but the demographics had changed. I found it quite a colorful place to be. After all,

I was with my dad, and there were always plenty of conversations for me to listen to.

At that particular time, my parents were again separated. I had grown quite used to my parents' arguments and the sudden departures of my father, though I didn't always know what spawned those rifts, however hard I tried to keep on top of things. I did know that no matter what happened, my dad always seemed to be trying his best to get my mother to take him back. I always felt so sad for my father, as we were close, and it was as though I could feel his heart aching.

On this particular Sunday, Dad was driving me back home after breakfast. When we arrived, he put the car in park. He reached over to give me a tearful hug and kiss and said to me, "Please tell Mommy to take me back." Hearing this as an innocent little girl, I experienced a deep pain that crushed me from within. My poor daddy was so desperate and hurting that he had turned to his little girl for help. I thought, *What on earth could I possibly do to help him?* I wanted to ease his pain, and I wanted my parents to get back together, but how could I possibly fix this and make it right when I was only a child? I was riddled with fear, sad for my daddy yet petrified at the thought of approaching my mother. I was torn because I felt as though my dad's fate rested in my hands. If I couldn't fix it, I would let him down.

His words weighed me down for so many years.

I found myself constantly replaying that scene in my head for the next few days while I tried to devise the right words to make my mother say yes without screaming at me for getting involved. While I was in school, I could barely concentrate. I didn't understand that it wasn't my job to be a mediator, that it wasn't normal for a child to be put in the middle of her parents' arguments. I never knew that children shouldn't be used as weapons.

A few days had passed, and I had summoned up the courage to confront my mother. I truly believed that if my mom knew how sad I was, she would reconsider her decision and let my dad come back home. I got home from school and waited for her to come home, and I approached her with my pathetic little face and said, "Mommy, please, can you let Daddy come home?" Tears streamed down my face as I looked up in anticipation and fear of her response.

She furrowed her brow in anger and slapped me hard across the face. "You mind your business," she snapped as my little hand fluttered up to the red mark on my cheek, and that was the end of the conversation as far as she was concerned. I, on the other hand, never forgot that day.

I'm not saying that my father was without blame during their breakups, but I suppose that with every time he was scorned by my mother, he felt the need to retaliate. However, not much time would pass before he could once again be seen begging to have her back. It was as though his longing for my mother outweighed his anger. The sadness in Dad's heart was always reflected in his eyes. It's funny—or sad, I should say—how certain memories stay with us no matter how much time has passed.

I was used like a pawn in a chess game between my parents, though I didn't realize this until I got older. I believed they couldn't see far enough beyond their own emotions to realize how much emotional damage they were inflicting on their children, particularly me. My mother intentionally manipulated and hurt people to get her way or make a point, whereas my father acted in retaliation for the internal wounds my mother inflicted upon him. He didn't realize that the actions he took against my mother created a ripple effect on his children, and some memories never seem to go away.

Tit for Tat

Their argument seemed vague to me, but it had sent my mother out of the house in a flurry. I was three, and we were living in our first house on Homewood Avenue, a pretty place with a big red oak tree on the front lawn. Even at three, I loved that house, our first family home.

It was nightfall. I had just finished helping my dad change my baby brother's diaper, Rory being one and a half years old. My dad went into the kitchen and emptied a drawer of its contents, placing the butter knives in a container. He asked me to come help him, and we went into the front vestibule, where I held the container of knives as he drew his hammer. I handed him the knives one by one as I curiously watched him insert them between the door and the jamb all around the doorframe.

I asked him, "What are we doing, Daddy?"

Pounding his hammer against the base of a knife, he replied, "We're locking Mommy out in case she tries to come home."

I didn't know this wasn't a common practice. I thought it was just something one did in response to an argument—it had been part of my conditioning to accept this as normal behavior. It wasn't long after this event that Dad sold our beautiful home with the red oak tree and we ended up moving to a little apartment on Bathurst Street without him.

Another of my fond memories involves the games my

parents played with one another during their separations. It seemed that any long separation wound up with my dad selling the family home. A few times, he also sold my mother's car right off the driveway without her knowledge. Sometimes, he would refrain from giving her money to live as part of her punishment. I suppose this was to make sure she wasn't out having a good time with his money, but it left us children caught in the crossfire.

We were still living in the little apartment. One day, my mother took me at age four, Rory at age three, and her pregnant self into a taxi. We were taken to the small fish store where my grandparents worked with my dad and his brother. When we got out of the cab, my mother roughly grabbed both of our little hands. She marched us inside, let go of our hands, and with venom in her voice, looked at my grandmother and said, "Here are two children for you. I can't feed them because your son won't give me money." She then sauntered out before anyone in the store could utter a word. I don't recall what happened after that, as it was the event itself that was etched into my memory. Eventually, after some days had passed, we were once again back at the apartment. I presume alternate arrangements were made.

Throughout our childhoods, we were used as messengers. If it wasn't my dad begging me to ask Mommy to take him back, it was my mother sending us off with threatening messages for my father whenever we would next be seeing him. However, it seemed that the birth of my little brother Robby brought a surprise reconciliation between my parents. We were moving to our new family home in Willowdale for a fresh start.

The home was a nice backsplit on Digby Court, a newer subdivision that drew many young families with children. My brothers and I played outside constantly when we lived there, as being outside was much more therapeutic than being in the house, which always seemed to be filled with discord. Surprisingly, we lasted for four years in that house, though my parents broke up at least twice more while we lived there. We had moved there when I was four, right after Robby was born, and two years later, even more surprisingly, my sister Melanie was born.

It's a funny thing, the baby business. My parents spent more time apart than together, yet babies were born. Surely some weak moments in reconciliation spawned our conceptions, but in retrospect, I have to say that we were all accidents. After Melanie was born, my mother had some gynecological problems that led her to have a full hysterectomy, though I'll spare the details of the state of mind this put her in. Suffice it to say that going through early menopause and the symptoms that came with it added to her already erratic temperament. In a strange kind of way, God has his reasons for everything. It was surely a blessing in disguise that there would be no more children born into our family, as we had enough to contend with. I certainly didn't need more siblings to take care of.

My Saving Grace

Some of the best times of my childhood were spent with my Aunty Sherry, my mother's older sister. She was my true sanity, the one I looked up to for guidance, and she always showed great concern and attention to me and my siblings. My aunt was beautiful, quite tall and very curvaceous. She had curly, strawberry-red hair and a winning smile, and her personality matched her looks: She was vibrant and could light up a room with just her presence. She loved to laugh. My aunt was my hero and the one constant in my childhood. I confided in her and was never afraid to ask her anything, though I never received answers to the questions I may have asked about my mother. If she promised to keep a secret, she never went against her word.

Aunty Sherry was truly a mother to all four of us, but she and I had a special bond, almost like a need that we both filled for each other. To me, she was a mother. To her, I was the child she never had. My aunt didn't marry until later in life, somewhere around forty. She stayed with us countless times during my mother's absences, and those were fun and happy times. I was always so excited when she stayed over. She made the best ham sandwiches, a simple concoction of ham and Wonder Bread smeared with mustard and butter.

When my aunt stayed over, she always shared my bedroom.

We would laugh in bed, and she would tell me wonderful stories. She also drove us to school and picked us up even though she felt anxious behind the wheel. We used to laugh about this, and she would tell us funny stories about driving. For example, she once told us that when she got off the exit ramp that went round in a circle, she would close her eyes because it made her dizzy. I always found that story so amusing, and back then I didn't really understand that she was just joking.

Men loved her, too, but she only had room in her heart for one person. Unfortunately, when she met my Uncle Neil, he was married—unhappily, but still married. Anyone who knew them knew they were one another's soul mates. It took about twelve years before they could be married, but they were crazy about each other until the day they died.

When I was a child, my Uncle Neil was around us a lot while they were dating, and I didn't know that he was otherwise married. It wouldn't have changed anything for me, because I grew to love him, too. They took me along on some of their dates, and a few times they even took me along to a supper club for dinner and dancing. How lucky I felt to be able to go to the grown-up club. My Uncle Neil used to dance with me and tell me to put my feet on top of his so that he could steer us across the floor. He was big and tall, not the handsomest of men, but he had a great sense of humor and always loved to make people laugh. He was just crazy about my Aunty Sherry.

Before they were married, I spent all the time I could with my aunt. She was my guide throughout my teenage years. Even after they married, my aunt and uncle came to visit us often, and I sometimes was allowed to go to their place and sleep over. I found it so ironic that my only aunt with no biological children was the one who had the most to teach and give.

Through the years, my mother and my Aunty Sherry would go through many bouts of not speaking to one another. I didn't know what these feuds were about, but I did know that my mother not talking to someone at any given time seemed to be standard. She was very bossy, hot-tempered, and terribly spoiled. She wouldn't hear anything that could knock her off her pedestal. In fact, most who knew her wouldn't even bother voicing a difference of opinion, as this would only lead to an argument that ended with my mother storming out of the room or banging down the phone.

My Aunty Sherry was the only one who ever stood up to my mother, calling her out on her behavior and taking her down a few rungs. It was, in fact, because of these common episodes that my mother would stop talking to my aunt. I was present many times for their falling-outs, and I always felt uncomfortably tense when an argument was brewing. My aunt's famous line was, "Lexi, stop being so dramatic and cut the shit."

I used to think my aunt was so brave to call my mother out. Of course, the same pattern ensued, with my mother stomping out and not talking to my aunt again for weeks, sometimes for months—a few times for years. This hurt me terribly: I knew I wouldn't be able to see my aunt, as she lived far away and I would have no way of getting to her if she wasn't allowed in our house. However, I was happy we could still speak on the phone, as these arguments had no impact on my love for Aunty Sherry.

Maid Service

When I was nine, I found some short-lived happiness. My parents had reconciled again, which meant I once again felt content. As was the pattern, we were moving again, and I suppose these fresh starts might have been an enticing factor that led my mother toward reconciliation. My dad had bought a big house not too far away from where we had lived on Digby Court. It was a brand-new subdivision, and ours was one of the first houses to be built. I remember this because it was scary to look out the window at night and see nothing but the black and barren land.

Our new home on Inglis Gate was so beautiful. We nick-named it the Whitehouse, as it had a grand circular driveway and leading up to the front doors were two white column posts on either side of the porch. There were many rooms and a fin-ished basement with a bar and sauna, but my favorite was the marble bathroom upstairs, which had a big oval bathtub with golden swan taps—by which I mean that the water flowed up and out through the neck of a gold swan. The house was quite modern for the late 1960s.

I was also very excited because the house had five bedrooms, which meant I was getting my own room, or so I thought. Even-tually I did, but only after a few years had passed. Apparently, the plan was that my sister and I would share a room and my brothers would share another. My parents had the big master and en-suite, which was quite something back then. This left two other bedrooms, referred to as the spare rooms.

We were going to get a maid. This was a dream come true for my mother, allowing her to have total freedom without having to worry about who would look after us while she was gone. Of course, having a maid meant that Mom wouldn't even have to do laundry or cook at all, though she seldom did anyway, as we already had a cleaning lady once a week. Life was grand with a "maid in the shade," as I liked to call it.

Well, as all good things come to an end, eventually so did the maid service.

*

Our first maid was Vera. She was not a very nice person, a skinny little woman who never had much to say. Honestly, what I remember about her most was that she loved to pick her nose. I knew she was a relative of one of my mother's friends' maids, and she came from an island in the Caribbean—I don't recall where because I really wasn't interested in her. My complaints about her went unheard, but a few months later she was let go by my mother, who was finding her personal things missing quite frequently. To her credit, the final straw for my mother was when she caught Vera pushing my little brother Robby.

Our next maid was Dolly, whom I loved. She was a big, heavy-set Jamaican woman who loved to laugh, and she gave me lots of attention. She was my buddy. She loved to play her reggae albums on our huge hi-fi stereo console, and I used to dance with her to her favorite song, "Stir It Up." She would play that song over and over and tell me interesting stories of life back home.

*

About two years had passed since we moved, and I was finding it difficult to sleep at night. My parents were constantly arguing, almost on a nightly basis. My radar would go off, and I would try desperately to hear what was being said behind their closed door, darting out of bed to get within hearing range. It was sometimes hard to get good information with the door shut, as their voices were muffled when they weren't shouting. I dared not stand too close to their door for fear it might open at any given moment with my dad storming out. These were the beginnings of yet another separation. I don't think I was trying to hear each word so much as the simple answer to a frightening question: Was my dad leaving us again?

I just had to know, because I didn't want to wake up to find that he was gone. The waiting and wondering were all-consuming for me, but my assumptions were correct. Once again, my father had been evicted by my mother. My cozy little respite in life had come to an end. Cutback time was approaching. Gone was the maid, my wonderful friend Dolly.

Tag . . . I was it.

*

My mother's social life had taken off exponentially after we moved to Inglis Gate. I can only imagine that this was the cause of the latest separation. She was at the racetrack, gambling with my dad's money and gallivanting at night with her acquaintances. Needless to say, with no maid, much of the burden fell on my shoulders. Heck, why not? I was almost eleven by then. I made all the beds, and I had to go straight home from school so I could first pick up my baby sister from kindergarten and then be home in time for my brothers. That also allowed me time to do some laundry and straighten up the house before making dinner. I didn't question my duties, because if chores weren't done and the house wasn't in order, I couldn't bear my mother coming home and screaming at me. After dinner, I did my homework. On the nights my mother stayed out late, which was often the case, she arranged for a babysitter to stay with us.

Ironically, at that time in my life, those weekend jaunts to my grandparents' house were almost a welcome relief from the daily grind. I looked forward to my mother's vacations because they were like a vacation for me, too, from chores and screaming. Sometimes it was my dad who stayed with us. He would actually move in for the week or however long my mother would be gone so that we had adult supervision at night in that big house. It was so nice to have dinner with my dad and watch TV together at night. Just knowing he was home with us was comforting.

Looking back, it truly amazes me how cleverly contrived my mother's plans were.

After a few years had passed, my parents once again miraculously reunited. My siblings and I were so happy to have our dad back. He wasn't the most active guy around, pretty much a homebody, but he was with us every night, and we were together. The best part about it for me was that I didn't have to feel the familiar sorrow that I had carried in my heart each time he drove off after a visit. I was mystified as to why, through all the years that my mother inflicted so much heartache on my dad, he continually wanted her back. The truth was that he was addicted to her beauty, and that seemed to take precedence over everything.

*

One day, when I was twelve, I came home from school and found my father's car in the driveway. As I walked into the house, I was curious as to what was going on, because he should have been at work. I wondered what I'd be walking into.

Dad was sitting at the kitchen table, just staring into space. I could hear my mother puttering around upstairs. I went over to my dad and said, "Hi, Daddy! What are you doing home so early?"

I will never forget the blank emptiness in his eyes when he looked up at me. He started to cry and withdrew into a childlike position, with fear and uncertainty in his eyes. He looked like a frightened little bird. The sight sent chills through my veins. My mother came down the stairs quickly when she heard my screams and cries along with my father's. I kept screaming, "Daddy doesn't know who I am!"

It was a fact: My father didn't recognize me. He had suffered a stroke at age thirty-eight. My mother rushed him to the hospital. I didn't even know how he had made it home from work or why an ambulance never came, but he was in the hospital for a few weeks. He was paralyzed on one side of his body, he couldn't speak, and he had lost his memory. I had never even heard of such a thing as a stroke, and being that Dad was only thirty-eight, I had never imagined that something so terrible could happen to him.

God had mercy on him. Miraculously, my father recovered and gained back full movement, speech, and memory. That horrifying day when I saw him like a scared little child sitting in the kitchen loomed deep in my memory for years. It was a different time back in 1971. Medicine, not as advanced then as it is today, was best for healing wounds or headaches, not for understanding the root cause of an illness or explaining how to prevent it. You healed and you carried on. My dad went back to his same old lifestyle, with its ups and downs and unhealthy habits.

The Last Time

When I was well into my fifteenth year, my maternal grandfather took very ill. He was then in his early seventies, and up until that time, he had been living much like a recluse. I had never seen him more than a couple of times a year. He lived downtown in one room of a boardinghouse, and he kept mostly to himself, always saying he didn't want to bother anyone or put anyone out. He lived on a pension, but he was a very proud man. Whenever we did see him, he was dressed immaculately in a shirt and tie. He was very well groomed and took pride in his appearance, with eyes bluer than the sky and a luxurious head of thick. white hair.

I really loved my Zaidy Goldhar, as we all affectionately called him, *Zaidy* being the Yiddish term for *grandfather*. Only at my mother's insistence would he occasionally come to visit us, though he never wanted to be picked up, as he felt the long drive to his house would create an inconvenience. Instead, he would take a few buses and make the half-mile walk to our house from the stop. He would stay over for the night or maybe two, and we would play gin rummy at night and drink tea together. If my mother left the car behind on her daily outings, Zaidy would drive me to school and come back later to pick me up. This was a treat for me, as the walk to school was about two and a half miles.

That year, my Zaidy was diagnosed with colon cancer. His life as he knew it, and his pride, had both disappeared, as the terrible ordeal left him with a colostomy bag and the humiliation that came along with it. The surgery left him with gangrene in his left leg, which had to be amputated. This was terrifying for all of us, but most importantly for him. At that point, he needed to be cared for, a further blow to his pride and independence. My mother was his only child with a house, and she instinctively informed my father that we were taking my grandfather in. My father was a very compassionate man and wouldn't have abandoned my grandfather in his time of need, but he sure had his reservations about how the situation would unfold.

The front den downstairs was emptied of its contents, becoming a bedroom with a hospital bed and a full-time nurse. After a few months had passed, my grandfather learned to take charge of his own colostomy bag and began to get a grasp on maneuvering his wheelchair around by himself. My parents then let the nurse go, as it had been quite expensive to maintain her services. I had acquired the added responsibility of babysitting my grandfather.

There were countless times I asked my mother if I could go out with my friends, and the answer was always, "No, you have to look after Zaidy." One day, after some months had passed, I was invited to spend the weekend with my friend Mandy and her family on their boat. I loved going out to their boat; I had been on it a few times, but only for the afternoon, so the invitation to go for a whole weekend was exhilarating to me.

I waited anxiously for my mother to come home that evening, all the while practicing conversations in my head, ways I could convince her to let me go for the weekend. When she got home, I broached the topic with great enthusiasm and excitement as I told her about the weekend plans. As I crossed my fingers, hoping for a positive response, my pulse raced in my throat in anticipation of the reaction I had braced myself for. She screamed out, "I told you no! You need to stay home and look after your grandfather." I went to my room, slammed the door, and cried for hours. Later that night, I heard it: the final argument, the last one my parents would have as a cohabitating couple.

This time, there were no muffled sounds, the words audible throughout the house. For the first time in my entire life, my father took a stand to my mother in my defense. He began by reminding her that I was just a child who had never enjoyed her childhood, that I had spent my entire life doing everything she asked of me. He shouted out, "Let her be with her friends and have a life of her own!" He also told her that I wasn't her personal maid or my grandfather's nurse. He wasn't really yelling, merely pleading with her to let me live my own life. I couldn't believe I was actually hearing all of it. The whole time my dad was trying to make my mother understand what she was doing to me, she tried to dominate the conversation with denial. Then came the last part of my father's sermon, words that would be forever embedded in my mind. He told my mother, in a very compassionate way, that the time had come for my grandfather to be put into a home so he could be looked after properly and so that I could have a life. It was as though an atomic bomb had gone off in my mother.

She screamed at the top of her lungs, "Get out! You don't care about my father—get out!" She didn't say a single thing about me, no remorse for what my father had accused her of. There was only the sound of my father emptying his drawers once again, getting ready to pack up and leave. That time, it was for good. Soon after, my Zaidy was put in a home, and not long after that, the cancer spread to his liver. He died within the year.

Saying Good-bye to the Family Home

My daddy had been gone from home for two years by the time I turned eighteen. Their most recent breakup had been the last, and our home had been sold. I was the only person left in the empty house. Everything was packed and gone—the only things left behind were memories. I reminisced over my short life. I had looked after my siblings, cleaned the house, done the laundry, made dinners. The kids were now old enough to take care of themselves.

I wiped my tears and took a last look around. This was the final chapter to my childhood, and when I turned to leave and put the key inside the door, I vowed to begin anew. The past would stay on the other side of the door, and I would be free. Or would I?

Reflections

Growing up is a search and rescue. We find a way to survive using what little skill we start out with, and only time and knowledge help us evolve into the people we become.

W e were all left with damage from our upbringing. The years that I had spent playing mommy had perhaps damaged my relationships with my siblings. I suppose I had been so busy doing my chores and trying to have some sort of a social life that I had never spent any quality time with my baby sister. There was a six-year age difference between us, a large gap for such young children.

However, no matter the dysfunction living in our house, we had all been brought up strictly and had turned into good kids. Perhaps the term "Mommy fearing" was more adequate. It hadn't even mattered that our mother wasn't around to make sure we behaved and followed her rules, because the fear of her wrath alone if we disobeyed her had been enough to keep us in line. It was almost like psychological warfare—we had all threatened one another through the years with the classic, "I'm telling Mommy!" and those threats had been enough to stop us in our tracks. If one of us were to get away with the occasional faux pas, that wrongdoer would almost certainly spend the next few days granting favors in order not to be ratted on.

As the years went by, the house rules eased up a bit. It became harder for us to continuously abide by the more old-fashioned restrictions, especially when our mother wasn't even home to enforce them. The tattling seemed to diminish, and the new set of lax rules gave my sister way more freedom than I had been entitled to at her age. I used to tell her she was lucky she didn't have to deal with all the crap that I had gone through, but looking back, she was no better off. Melanie was left on her own to grow up. Thankfully, my brother Rory kept her under his wing. My sister, being the youngest, had even less parental guidance than I had received, and Rory was like a father figure to her. He had adored Melanie since the day she was born, and he was always—and still is to this day—her protector.

I have one outstanding impression of my sister as a little girl: She had a dire need for love and affection. We all craved it, of course, but my brothers and I had different ways of displaying our needs. When she was very small, my sister went through a long phase in which she had a persistent good-bye ritual. This applied to everyone, from relatives to friends who may have been visiting our home. Whenever someone was leaving, whether it was just out for the night, going to the store, or saying good-bye, my sister would start crying. She needed whoever was leaving to give her a kiss, but not just once. She would ask for another kiss and yet another and cry her little heart out as though she would never again see that person, and this ritual could go on for a good twenty minutes. It makes me so sad to think about it now. I didn't understand it when I was young, but it was a desperate cry for love and a sign of her fear of abandonment.

It wasn't until I moved out and got my own apartment that my sister and I developed a friendship, as only then did I begin to take my role as a big sister more seriously. By then my mother was renting a townhome, and my siblings were living there with her. They were still pretty much on their own, and I was living the dream at eighteen. I believe my sister had way more freedom than a girl of twelve should have been permitted, but I had no control. I was grateful that she never did anything to get in serious trouble, as she had been unleashed and set free into the world with hardly any guidance at such a young age. Melanie also took on the role of the little Suzy Homemaker. Although she was the youngest, she took over where I had left off in the household.

When she felt she couldn't take any more of my mother's antics, she would flee to my apartment. My mother would then call me, freaking out about my sister, as she so often used to rant to any one of us about the others. I did stand up to her, though—after all, I no longer lived under her roof, and she could no longer boss me around, but my insides still stirred with fear of the wrath she had so often inflicted on me. I told her she should just be grateful my sister ran away to my place and not somewhere out on the streets, and that usually put an end to those conversations.

My brother Rory and I are fourteen months apart. When we were little, we were as tight as two bugs in a rug. We were each other's best friends, as we were the only real constants in each other's lives. When I was four and he was three, we were living in that little apartment on Bathurst Street, and we used to make up little games and play together all the time. Dad wasn't living with us at the time, so a neighbor, Katie, looked after us often. Rory and I were good kids with curious minds. We tended to get into mischief, as little ones often do, but this was understandable, as we played with little supervision. I usually brainstormed these good ideas.

One thing was true: We sure did love our treats. In the living room, there was a high table with two drawers, and inside one of those drawers, I could usually find some candies, sometimes even chocolate bars. One day, I decided we should have some chocolate, so I grabbed a stool and climbed up so I could reach the drawer. I grabbed what seemed like a chocolate bar but in fact turned out to be a bar of Ex-Lax. Thinking back on that day, I have to wonder: what on earth was that doing in the junk drawer anyway? Needless to say, we divided it up, and I, being the one to split it, instinctively hogged more than my share. I remember that after eating it and getting caught by my mother, I had to take some big ugly charcoal pills and spent much of the day on the toilet.

Another time, I wanted some Chiclets, tiny gum that came in little packets in an array of colors. My favorites were the orange ones. That particular day, there weren't any Chiclets around, but I did find something small and orange to suffice, and being four, I didn't know any better. I didn't share any with my brother, but that small bottle of baby aspirin led me to one scary visit to the hospital to get my stomach pumped.

I had quite the imagination, and aside from using it to find snacking alternatives, I used it to take me to happy places when my real life was full of unhappy moments. I used to dream of family outings, and I would pretend I was a movie star, or I would play with my dolls as though they were real people. Those things kept me happy. I also used to love watching the TV show *Bewitched*. I was so fascinated by the fact that the main character could crinkle up her nose and twitch it to make anything happen. I would stand in front of a mirror for hours and twitch my nose, wishing so hard and really believing I could make something happen. When nothing happened, I would just live my wish out in my imagination. I was so precocious and quite a little Chatty Cathy.

Rory, on the other hand, had grown to be a quiet little boy, and as the years went by, he seemed to acquire a lot of inner anger. I'm not a psychoanalyst, but I'm quite sure my brother's anger stemmed from his desire for attention from my father, who wasn't with us much when we were small, and from my ever-absent mother, whose love and affection my brother also craved. I think this was very frustrating for him because, despite what we realized about our mother as we got older, he idolized her and yearned for her attention.

As we grew into our teens, Rory and I seemed to drift apart. We locked horns at every opportunity, and his internal anger had somehow become directed toward me. I'm still unsure why this happened, as we now choose not to speak about those days. I suspect this deep-rooted anger toward me stemmed from the fact that I had taken the reins growing up, which may have caused Rory to resent me for replacing the mother he missed. It seemed as though all the love my brother kept inside him was given to my little sister. Since the day she was born, he had always said, "She's my baby," as if she had finally brought him something of his very own to love.

I know that we were all affected by our childhood in different ways. Thankfully, as we got older, Rory and I mended our relationship. Even though he is fourteen months younger than me, I now fondly refer to him as my big brother.

Growing up, it seemed as though the four of us formed teams. Rory and Melanie were very close, and Robby and I had our own special relationship. When Robby was born in our little apartment on Bathurst Street, my parents were still not yet back together. I assume my parents had attempted another reconciliation, or perhaps just had a weak moment when Robby was conceived, but nonetheless, Robby was born, and he was *my* baby.

As a child, Robby gave off an angelic energy, and people couldn't help but be taken with him. Robby was a gentle, meek little boy with the biggest blue eyes and hair white as snow. All the adults fawned over him, more than over any of us. As it turned out, Robby grew into a clone of my father, and he definitely inherited my dad's meek and mild disposition.

When Robby was three, there was a horrifying incident concerning him. Somehow, he found his way outside one morning and disappeared. I came home from school that day and found my mother and my Aunty Sherry in hysterics on the front lawn. I remember hearing their terrible, howling sobs. A police car was parked on the driveway, and my dad was out searching with several people who had gathered to help look for Robby. I couldn't fully comprehend that *my* baby could disappear, but I did know enough to feel that sickening pit in my stomach as I joined in the cries. I was worried to death that I would never again see my baby brother. There was nobody to comfort me in those moments, as emotions were running high and we were all consumed by thoughts of my missing brother.

I truly believe in my heart that the only reason he was found safe and unhurt, by the grace of God, was that society was different in the early 1960s. My mother's cousin found him, and Lord only knows how a toddler could wander the streets a mile away all day and not be hit by a car or kidnapped. It also puzzled me that nobody saw this little boy wandering around unattended in his little training pants and T-shirt. It still brings tears to my eyes as I write, remembering that horrific day. As I got older and realized the severity of that incident, I never stopped wondering how it could even have happened—but I eventually realized that I did know. Rory and I had gone to school that morning, leaving from the side door. The door never locked, and the handle only needed a light touch before that door would swing open. We left, and Robby was up, wandering around by himself while my mother was sleeping. This was how terrible things could happen. When God brought Robby back to us, I vowed that I would always take care of him.

Through the years, Robby and I were very close. He was such a good boy, very quiet, not mischievous as Rory and I were. Everybody loved Robby, and he always did whatever I asked of him, even putting up with my crazy little compulsive quirks. I was always terrified to take a shower because I had a fear of the unknown, and perhaps a scary monster would be hiding behind the curtain, waiting for me when I got out. I suppose that was part of my grand imagination, though perhaps watching *Psycho* had not been such a good idea, either. Nonetheless, Robby would always fulfill my requests. For years, he would stand outside the bathroom door without complaint until I was done in the shower. He never questioned me—he just did whatever I asked of him.

Home

I stepped out of my childhood, reached out my hand, and grabbed the life that was rightfully mine.

It had been almost two years since my father moved out for the last time. He was no longer living like a nomad, moving back and forth from our home to his parents' home, or to motels, or between month-to-month rentals. My dad was settled, living in a beautiful apartment in a gated community. He had resolved himself to finally move on, and there was no repairing my parents' relationship after he had stood up to my mother that fateful day. My father knew my mother well enough to know that her twisted interpretation of his words was the only one she would believe as the truth.

Dad wasn't made of money, so it was no surprise that the time had come to sell the family home on Inglis Gate. After all, there was no need for him to pay a mortgage on a big house that he would no longer be living in. Besides, he had his own rent to pay along with all the other bills, as well as giving a generous allowance to my mother. Meanwhile, I had moved into my own apartment. It was my sanctuary, and I was ecstatic to finally be on my own, living my own life by my own rules. I felt so lucky to have this fabulous apartment, which had been almost impossible to obtain.

In the end, it had been through a stroke of genius that I got the apartment, all because of a plan hatched by my dad and my Aunty Sherry. During the time that the family home was for sale, my aunt was a rental agent for a very prominent apartment complex. There were three buildings to this complex, called Roseview Circle. In 1978, Roseview Circle was the "in" place to live, mostly inhabited by working singles. There were long waitlists to get an apartment there, as many professionals seemed to be migrating to the area. My aunt had worked it out with my dad and told him it was time I went out on my own and started *living*. Naturally, I wasn't on the waitlist, and my dad agreed to pay my rent for me until I could get on my feet. Those were to become the best years of my life.

I was so happy. It was an added bonus that my aunt was working right downstairs in the office, and I would often pop down and have little visits with her when she wasn't too busy. She would also come up to my place for dinner many times when she was working at night. Just when I thought it couldn't get any better, my aunt got me a part-time job as a receptionist in the recreation center of the building. This worked out fabulously for me, as my job was one flight of stairs away from home, and I was also going to university part time to study music.

Music was my inspiration for everything in life, and I had been gifted with a beautiful singing voice. I was taking classical voice training, and my aspiration at the time was to become a singer. I concentrated my efforts on that path for a few years, doing some gigs with my band friends. I also recorded a demo tape for circulation, but in those days it was really tough to make it in the recording industry without the right connections. Eventually, I gave up the dream.

One day, my father dropped by to visit me at work. We sat and chatted for a while, as it happened to be quiet in the center while he was there. Suddenly, my dad laid a set of car keys on my desk, saying, "I want you to be safe, so I bought you a car."

I was beside myself with joy. He took me outside to see my shiny, new, white Mustang, and I hugged and kissed him as though I had just won the lottery. I could see the pride in my father's face when he saw the excitement radiate in mine. Then we went out for a quick spin.

Up to that point in my life, I had been a loner. In high school, I hadn't really cared about getting involved in any activities, as the school I had gone to was out of my district and I would walk a half mile before taking three buses to get there and back every day. My parents had sent me to that school because it was known for its academic program, and I happened to be quite smart. It seemed, though, that all the other kids in that school had known each other since junior high and had already formed cliques. My only real friends there, Mandy and her sister, had migrated to that school as well. I did, however, become friends with a girl named Cori, and we're still friends today. Cori was a social butterfly, and we always had fun together. We went to Miami once together when I was twenty-one—a big step for her, as she was just finishing high school and I was already living on my own. We had a blast, and I could probably write another book about the shenanigans we got into on that trip.

It was only when I began working at the rec center that my life really began to change. I met my best friend, though the term "best friend" can hardly describe what Zandra became. She was a mentor, a guide, a sister, and practically a mother to me. She was my soul sister. We were both the same age, yet she had a certain something that made me look up to her.

Zandra worked as a lifeguard up at the pool in the rec center, while I worked downstairs in the office. When there were no guests, Zan and I would chat with one another on the linked phones between our offices, and this was where our lifelong friendship began. Little did we know that we had both come from similarly dysfunctional families. Ironically, we came from totally different backgrounds yet had lived parallel lives.

Zandra had a beautiful soul and also happened to be a strikingly sexy girl, yet with the modest way she carried herself, one would think she wasn't aware of her beauty. Zandra was Slavic, born in Yugoslavia. Her parents came from politically opposite sides of the country, Croatia and Serbia, and perhaps those were the beginnings of her family's dysfunction. When Zan and I became friends, she still had her natural brown hair, having yet to become the blonde bombshell she is today. At the time, I was the natural blonde, but she had the whole package: a beautiful spirit, equally beautiful on the outside. She had long brown hair, sexy blue cat eyes, and a body to kill for.

When I met Zandra, I was a very insecure person. I still carried the neuroses I had acquired as a child, and I'd had a terrible inferiority complex ever since my awkward teen years. I had always wanted to be pretty, yet no matter what people told me, I never acknowledged my beauty. My complex was similar to that of someone who has been fat all her life and suddenly becomes thin only to see the same old fat person staring at her from the mirror.

During my teen years, I had very low self-esteem. I had never been complimented on my appearance or encouraged by anyone, as I was rather average and nobody had shown me how to put myself together. I had no idea how to apply makeup other than what I had tried to learn by watching my mother before she shooed me out of her space. I didn't even know what a period was until I'd already had it for four months in a row, too petrified to tell my mother for fear I would get in trouble. It scared me—I thought there was something really wrong with me, yet I was afraid to tell anyone. Finally, my mother caught me one day with blood seeping through my jeans, as the paper towels I had stuffed down my pants weren't enough to stop the flow. She didn't explain anything to me, just went to the store to buy me some Kotex pads and told me to use them.

Zandra helped me come out of my shell and taught me to appreciate my true worth. I learned from her that it was okay to express emotion and say the words "I love you" to someone instead of keeping it inside. She taught me all about the girlie stuff I hadn't learned at home, and she introduced me to a whole new world. This was a world that invited me to learn new things, new cultures, make new friends, find fulfillment. She also taught me self-esteem. To this day, thirty-four years later, we remain best friends. We've shared a million miles of laughter and tears, heartbreaks, losses, victories, birthdays, weddings, divorces, funerals, and distance. We've weathered so much together that not even the great ocean that now separates us could ever come between us.

When I wasn't occupied with Zandra, I frequented a little Italian cafe not far from where I lived. It was a regular hangout for several young adults like me. I had joined the real world of socializing, and it felt good to grow up and come out of my withdrawn personality. I was just getting used to my new self-esteem, and I still wasn't used to accepting a compliment. While living at home, I had become somewhat chubby, which stemmed from my nervousness growing up, but the weight seemed to disappear once I moved away.

I had befriended the owner of the cafe. When I went there, he and I often had grand conversations about life and everything under the sun. His name was Manny, and he was a gentle man, not particularly handsome but a beautiful person within. As the months went by, Manny developed a great affection for me, and I found it exciting that someone was actually captivated by me. Manny was married—unhappily, as I learned through the years, but nevertheless married. He was also about twenty-eight years my senior. Ironically, this did not faze me. We developed a relationship, which suited me well. I was too young and unaware of possible repercussions, and quite frankly, the situation was perfect for me because I somehow had the idea that it was safe: safe because I didn't have to commit, safe because I had known all my life that I never wanted to marry. All I had learned of marriage came from my parents, and the thought of it just didn't appeal to me.

Our relationship lasted for a few years, off and on. It was almost as though I was living a double life. It was a private relationship, and I otherwise acted as though I was single. I worked, I had a great social life, and I would see Manny at his cafe. His home was also quite near mine, and we would share time together at my apartment later in the evenings, after he closed the cafe. I learned a lot from him about the world and life, but most of all, I learned what it felt like to be completely loved.

During those early years in my twenties, I still kept in contact with my dad. We had dinner together twice a week, once on Friday night at his parents' and once for Chinese food to catch up. I never told my father about my relationship with Manny, as I knew it wouldn't please him to know I was seeing an older married man. I didn't see the need to tell him about something that would only hurt him, as it was keeping me happy at the time and was never going to end in marriage. My mother knew about my relationship with Manny because of some social circles she and I shared, but I made her promise never to tell my father.

*

I used to go nightclubbing with my girlfriends a few times a week. I never saw much of my mother, but she too went clubbing at a few of the places I frequented. It was odd to think that after the tumultuous relationship I'd had with my mother through life, we were now socializing in the same places. I suppose, at the time, it was a strange novelty; we hadn't spent much time together as I was growing up, but we were now sharing glasses of wine and attention from men. My mother was still very beautiful, and I had grown into my looks by then.

My mother had never looked her age, and nobody ever took her for more than ten years older than me. In fact, we were often asked if we were sisters. She relished these comments, but sometimes she'd set her eyes on a man I had been getting to know, and when her attention wasn't reciprocated, I could feel her resentment and jealousy in my bones. This became more apparent when she was drinking. Her tongue seemed to sharpen immensely, and she became sarcastic and cutting. I could almost see the little green monster rearing its head, crying, "I'm here! Look at me! I'm the fairest of them all!" It was a very unsettling feeling, knowing my mother felt she had to compete with me for male attention.

I would often exchange dysfunctional family stories with Zandra, and one time I even asked her if I was imagining things. Could it really be possible that my mother was becoming jealous of her own daughter? It sickened me that my mother considered me nothing more than competition.

One night, when I was about twenty-two, I was sitting at home in my apartment when I received a phone call from my dad. All he said was this: "I'm just calling to tell you that your mother called me and told me about your relationship with some married guy." There was a heavy silence for a moment, and then he added, "I just want you to know you're no longer my daughter. I still love you. Good-bye."

My world was shattered. I hung up the phone, completely devastated. I remember sitting on my couch with tears streaming down my cheeks, looking out the window at the empty street. My foremost feelings were of anger toward my mother. Why did she have to tell him? Why did she have to hurt him so badly with that information? What did she have to gain from this? Sure, she wanted to get back at me for perhaps having too much fun. Most of all, I knew she felt that I was stealing her limelight when we were out together. This disgusted me—an attack from my own mother in retaliation for her jealousy, her broken promise to never reveal my secret, and a revelation that severed the closeness I shared with my father. She didn't care that she had broken his heart once again. She just wasn't happy, so why should anyone else have been?

After I dwelled on my mother's actions, I began digesting my disbelief that my dad could disown me. How did that even happen? How could my dad just disregard our life, all the years I had looked out for him, all because of a drunken phone call from my mother? I cried and cried for hours, weeping for the pain my mother had so intentionally inflicted on my father. I wept for the loss of my dad, and I cried even more as I replayed the conversation over and over in my head. *I still love you. Good-bye.* His words had hit me hard because as close as Dad and I were, I never had any recollection of him ever telling me he loved me. It had been an unspoken understanding, as the words "I love you" were just not spoken in my family.

I'm quite sure his inability to say those words was a result of his emotionally challenged parents. Once again, we are products of where we come from. One either follows the pattern or breaks free, as I did. By telling me he still loved me, he confirmed what I had known all my life: he had loved me without words. Hearing him say that seemed to make everything that much sadder. I had longed to hear those words in our everyday lives for years, but he spoke to me over the phone as though the words had already been said.

In the weeks after my separation with my father, my heart was heavy with sorrow for him. Besides the fact that I no longer had my dad in my life, I was more concerned about how he was doing, because I knew that despite what he said, I had been the apple of his eye since I was born. I had already lashed out at my mother for being so callous, and I had disowned her myself. I felt no remorse. My siblings called me regularly to inform me how sad my dad was, and my sister repeatedly told me he was so broken that he looked like he was going to have a heart attack. This pained me, as he already had a bad heart and had already suffered a stroke. I worried for him, but I was also grieving for myself. I was the one who had been disowned, and nobody seemed to care about how I felt.

About four months later, I was home one evening, getting ready to go dancing, when the phone rang. It was my dad, and he caught me completely off guard. He sounded very nervous, and I listened in anticipation. My father took a huge step by taking back his words, telling me he was sorry for his harsh reaction and that I needed to understand how the news had been relayed to him by my mother. He told me he realized the information should never have been able to destroy our relationship, and I told him that what he knew could never change what we shared. Between sobs, I blurted out, "I still love you. Good-bye?" Those were the words that had hurt me the most. I told him I couldn't recall him ever saying he loved me, so his admission had been huge, and he apologized. With tears shed, we both agreed to move forward and put the whole thing behind us, never mentioning it again—and we honored that promise.

As the months turned into years, I still received those phone calls from my siblings, but they became pleas to call my mother. I didn't want any part of it. Some calls may have come from the genuine concern of my siblings, but I knew that others were made at the urging of my mother. There were many calls. My sister once called and said, "Mom is living on Valium, and sometimes she says she's going to kill herself," but I had no intention of talking to her, and her threats to kill herself had grown stale.

My wounds were very deep and still raw. I couldn't forgive her for putting my father through that ordeal. She'd had nothing to gain from it—and least of all from her betrayal to me. Her threats were like crying wolf. I had been through a lifetime of her dramatics and her Valium dependency and her suicidal threats to get what she wanted. I also hated that she had ensnared my siblings and made them worry that she might one day follow through on her threats. This was her usual arsenal in her search for attention.

Almost two years went by before I came face-to-face with my

mother again. I suppose I caved under the worry, or perhaps I felt as though enough time had passed and I should release my mother from her punishment. I halfheartedly mended fences with her, but not without reprimanding her for the situation, telling her what a terrible thing she had done to me and especially to my father. I also told her we would move on—but I still couldn't forgive her.

Self-Analysis

I thought all the years I had allowed myself to take orders and be disciplined by guilt were my duty as a child: adherence to the code of respect.

O n many nights I would sit on my couch in my peaceful apartment and ponder life, not so much where I was going but where I had come from. I was finally living in contentment, on my own, with no more fears or anxieties, for I had left those behind. I felt free. Now that I had peace of mind, I could clearly look back and assess my life, and things became so much more apparent when I could step out of the box and look in.

One night in particular, I was lying on the couch, listening to music. I often did this to relax and collect my thoughts, letting my mind take me where it might. I would also write little blurbs or poems about whatever was at the forefront of my mind at the time. That night, the subject, as was often the case, was my mother. I really began to dissect the events in my life starting from childhood. Because I was older now, I could piece together the answers to some of the questions that had riddled me as a child. It was as though I were reliving my life in my mind like it had happened to someone else.

The years of studying my mother began to make sense to me

as I filled in the gaps in my knowledge with what I had learned over time. As a child, many things didn't make sense to me, and some things I never even questioned. I grew to understand how well my mother had orchestrated her life, as well as mine. When I was younger, I had wanted to emulate her, to have her life—and who wouldn't have wanted that? It was a grand life. We were sent to our grandparents' home every weekend, and my mother came and went as she pleased. Nobody ever told her what to do or what not to do. She was so beautiful that men swooned over her, and she knew it, craved it, and used it. She was in such dire need of constant attention that she had to be in the limelight wherever she was. She had to have the best of everything so as to ensure that nobody else could outshine her. It was in her DNA. She used her beauty as a weapon.

To my father, my mother's beauty was a drug. As I got older, I questioned why, for so many years, he would continually want to get back together with her. I just couldn't fathom what he was getting out of it, as from where I stood, all he got was heartache. I can't even recall my mother ever showing affection toward my father. He gave her everything she wanted, but she didn't want him. She had lured him in with her beauty, and I was a premeditated way to get my father to marry her. I could understand that my mother had been poor as a child and that my dad, who came from a financially stable family, had to have been quite appealing for a young, struggling, beautiful girl. He was an opportunity for her to make a good life for herself, and his soft-spoken, meek nature coupled with his attraction to her beauty made pursuing her irresistible to him.

My mother had a knack for expanding the truth and making things appear much more grandiose than they really were. She also had a knack for creating stories and living as though they were actual truths, never backing down from her beliefs. Delusional and narcissistic, she lived in her own denial and expected everyone to believe her. Those who knew the truth never dared call her out on anything, except perhaps my Aunty

Sherry. I had grown to understand that the facade my mother put on display actually stemmed from her deep-seated insecurities. I think her unhappy childhood, which she never spoke of, made her determined to make a good life for herself, and nobody was going to get in her way. She came from nothing, with just the gift of beauty, and she very calculatingly used that to her full advantage.

I could never understand why my mother wouldn't admit that I had been conceived out of wedlock. It was as though the truth could have tarnished her reputation, a reputation she had made up for herself. I had questioned my father for years about why the math didn't add up, but he always gave me the same answer: He would chuckle and say, "Go ask your mother." I could see right through it, as I knew my father so well, but he knew whom he would have to answer to if he told me. When I did ask my mother, the answer was just too far-fetched for me to believe, even as a child. Her story was and remained the same throughout my entire life: My parents were actually married a year before their registered anniversary date. According to her, they were so in love that they had a secret wedding before the real wedding, which was two months after my conception. I still laugh at this fantastic story. I confirmed several times over that this was bullshit, but my mother stuck to her story even after the truth was uncovered. That was just who she was.

*

I continued to dig deep into my subconscious to find answers to the questions that troubled me. I reminisced over the countless weekends I had spent at my grandparents' home, weekends that had provided guilt-free babysitting services and allowed my mother her personal freedom. When I had finally told my grandparents that we wouldn't be spending weekends at their house anymore, my overwhelming feeling of freedom trumped my anxiety at delivering the news. Surprisingly, they got over it just fine. I'm sure they expected that the time would eventually come, and I had already heard whispers that it hadn't been their idea to have us four there every weekend in the first place. As I looked back, I realized that having four rambunctious children around had to have been an imposition on their quiet, sedentary, religious lifestyle.

Nevertheless, we didn't abandon them completely. For many years after we stopped spending weekends at my grandparents' home, the four of us children and my dad continued to go there for Friday-night dinners. It was standard and expected, but as far as I was concerned, it was an inconvenience for my newly established social life. I really only continued going for the opportunity to spend time with my father. I knew I was just going through the motions of this ritual to appease his parents, because there was never any love in their home. I would constantly air my grievances to my father about how I just knew that his parents didn't care for me and that I had never felt in my element around them, and though he constantly professed that this was nonsense, he and I both knew it was the truth. However, my dad always turned my complaints around by making jokes to lighten the mood. One of his favorite sayings about going to his parents' house was, "Let's eat it and beat it." He always made me laugh.

My thoughts shifted to my mother's countless absences throughout my childhood. I finally allowed myself to sift through those memories, wanting to find answers to the many questions I had deep down in my soul. I felt it was time to bring them to the surface and put the facts where they belonged. When I was six, when I used to take Rory to kindergarten and then pick him back up, my responsibilities had become apparent. Those were the days when "listening at the stairway" kicked in. My father wasn't living with us then, and lying there on the couch in my apartment, I suddenly remembered a male friend of my mother who sometimes came over.

I had always felt uncomfortable when he was around. He never did anything wrong, but I used to wonder why he could be at our home when my father wasn't allowed. I was too young to know it at the time, but my mother was actually seeing this man. Over the next few years, my mother took up her hobby of going to the racetrack, where she could gamble and get the attention she craved. She would get all gussied up and stand out in a crowd. Her presence commanded attention, and that was a drug for her. When she spoke, she had to make herself seem more than what she was. I used to watch her around people, and back then I had thought she was some kind of icon. Only as I grew up did I realize how desperate she was for constant attention.

I thought back to those summer holidays we spent in Fort Erie. Putting together the pieces of the past, I realized that taking us kids there on summer vacation was ideal for my mother. It was called our vacation, but in essence it was hers, and we were taken care of by someone else. She had her friends at the same motel and, of course, arranging for two rooms and a babysitter was a clever plan. It was obvious why there was no need for my father to be around.

My dad gave her beautiful things: homes, jewelry, and money to set the status for her ongoing social life. It was quite evident that men would do anything for her and that women envied her. I had noticed that my mother didn't have many female friends. Most women were acquaintances from her social circle, and she always had to one-up them in their presence. This was just something about her: No matter what and how much she had, she always had to make herself appear better than someone else so she could feel empowered. It really amazed me that some people actually wanted to befriend her. Maybe it was exciting to follow such a commanding presence, but I was sure that many people could see right through her.

It was at that time, as I was reliving my past, that I reached a turning point in my life. I promised myself that I would never be like my mother. From my youngest years right through to my teens, I had watched my mother hurt people with her sharp tongue, yet I too had been entranced by her beauty. Being young, I hadn't fully understood the true meaning of some situations or their repercussions—I had learned all I knew from her, and I had always thought I wanted to be glamorous, to have men fall to my feet at my beck and call. However, after all of my reflection that night, I realized this couldn't have been further from the truth.

I began to think about the patterns of people's lives. Yes, we are products of our environments, but we still have choices. We can either follow what we know best or take a fork in the road and go in another direction. I clearly realized that I wanted to take the fork. I too was becoming an attractive girl, but I had something different: I had an education and compassion; I had honesty and integrity. I didn't have it in me to better myself at another's expense or to use people to climb ladders. I also had a lot of love for those in my life. I didn't need to use weapons of manipulation. I didn't want a man to want me only for my looks.

That was the day I realized how very sorry I felt for my mother. As for my father, I had felt sorry for him my whole life. He just couldn't see past my mother's physical beauty, and I began to see him as one of her many conquests. As I put my life in perspective, all the emotional turmoil I had endured came to the forefront, and I realized how far I had come. I was wise beyond my years and had seen a lot more in my young life than most children should. I hadn't been given any guidance. After all, my parents had both been so young when they married that they didn't bring any real experience with them. Having both come from emotionally inept families, they didn't know how to raise children. My mother had lost her own mother at a young age, leaving her to fend for herself, and my dad's parents were such emotionless and private people that I wonder how they raised their children without knowing love and compassion.

My parents trekked through by trial and error, as I suppose many families did back then. Unfortunately, error was the front-runner when it came to raising children. With those thoughts in mind, I made a promise to myself that I would never, ever be like my mother. I wanted my beauty to shine through from the inside. I wanted peace and harmony. I wanted to come out of my shell and start speaking up about my feelings. Most of all, I wanted to be able to say "I love you," those three powerful little words I had barely heard in my childhood, whenever I felt the urge to let someone know. I had a lot of love in my heart, and I had already learned how valuable friendship was. It was so freeing to be capable of loving and to be loved in return.

Married Men Are Safe

He was like an Adonis. With his deep-green eyes and his warm smile, he stole a piece of my heart.

Another year had passed since my night of reflection. I was happy, and my social circle was expanding. I had really grown into myself, becoming more confident and learning about my true self-worth—I had also only just begun to realize that I was attractive and that men were paying attention to me. I had a hard time deciding what I wanted to do in life, so I seemed to change careers every few years, but I did so happily because I was free in the knowledge that I had the ability to choose what I wanted to be in life.

At twenty-one, I decided to take a night course and become a travel agent. This seemed only fitting for me, because I loved to travel. During that time, I had been managing a women's clothing store for a friend and loving it. When I became a certified travel agent, I decided to stay in retail but also became an outside agent, working with a travel agency. I had befriended the man who owned the agency while I was in school, and this worked out perfectly for me, as I could market myself and take my clients' bookings to his agency. I loved the travel agency course, fascinated by geography, which had seemed to hold no interest for me in high school. I made some money doing this, but being an agent afforded me the chance to go on a few little vacations almost free of charge, and I think my true motives were probably inspired by these travel perks.

By that time, I had outgrown Manny. When we met, Manny had been a gift to me and my self-esteem, but I was experiencing real life now, and my world had become very socially active outside the perimeters of my relationship with Manny. I had been frequenting another cafe—a hangout, so to speak—in my spare moments, and I was making a whole new set of friends and acquaintances. My social calendar was buzzing, and life was great. Zandra was still my best friend in the world. At the time, she was married to her high school sweetheart and living only blocks away from my apartment. On the weekends, I would get together for adventures with her and her husband, Gavin. We were like the three musketeers.

By that time, the women's wear store had closed down, and I was looking for more work. I had recently met Bill—who owned a photography company—at a party, and though we dated for a few months, I was getting bored and the romance had fizzled out. However, we remained friends, and he offered me a job selling family portraits. This job often took me on the road, with long hours, lots of driving, and many lonely nights in cheap motels across the province, nothing to fill my time besides paperwork from my sales. I did this for about a year and made a lot of money, but eventually I felt burned out and lonely, and the money no longer outweighed the grind. Bill was kind enough to give me an office job, which was where I met my other best friend, Brianna—or Bri, as I affectionately called her.

Bri shared office space with us, as her boss was Bill's partner in a different division of the company. We chatted often and discovered that we lived a block away from one another. We decided to carpool to work and take turns driving, and that was when we became best friends. I was so blessed to have two best friends, and even luckier that they both liked one another without any jealousy. Bri and I were at each other's houses almost daily for years. She was married, and going to her house had given me a sense of family and some good home-cooked meals. For Bri, my apartment was an escape from the daily grind, a place to relax.

Bri was soft-spoken and easy to be with, and she had a heart of gold. She was very slim, with long, tightly curled hair that she fought on a daily basis. She always hated that her hair could grow enormously big with any change in the weather, so she used lots of product to ensure that her curly hair would stay obedient and un-frizzed. I, on the other hand, would laugh because my hair was so straight that I had to get perms to give it any life. Bri was a pretty girl, though she would never acknowledge her looks. In fact, she also had low self-esteem back then, and I constantly gave her the encouragement she needed to see how beautiful she really was. I suppose Zandra had taught me well.

We laughed a lot and confided our deepest, darkest secrets to one another. Bri was always there for me when I needed her, which was mostly always. She was Italian, and I had already begun learning the language from my other friends. It came in handy for me to know the language, especially at the cafes I frequented, where men would make comments thinking I couldn't understand what they were saying. At the time, I only seemed to be interested in Italian men. I don't know if it was their charm or their good looks that attracted me, but I always thought they were just so romantic.

It was the early eighties then, and I had a full, exciting life, great friends, and lots of dates. I was making just enough money to allow me to indulge in my weakness for clothes shopping, my social activities, some groceries, and rent. What else did a girl need? I also had friends in the clothing business, which allowed me to buy at great discounts. I had become quite a fashion plate by then, perhaps because I had been so insecure growing up, feeling unattractive and chubby, that I was determined to make the most of my looks. Getting my own apartment and living on my own, I learned to eat healthier and focused on becoming my best self. I was no longer chubby and had grown nicely into my looks, thanks mostly to Zandra, who had taught me all about beauty aids and aesthetics. In fact, Zandra had become a licensed aesthetician by that time.

If I ever found myself short on cash, Bri stepped up and lent me money, which I always paid her back. Back then, it didn't cost a girl a fortune to go out to a nightclub. I loved to go dancing with my girlfriends, and I went twice a week—sometimes three times—for years. We loved music and dancing. Sure, we were hit on by tons of men, but that was half the fun. We danced and let them buy us drinks, and had fun together, but when the night was over we always went home as we came—together, just the girls. I had a theory that I stuck by: I would never go out with a guy I met at a bar. This worked for me.

I used to smoke back then, and I always bought my cigarettes at the local greasy spoon, just up the street from where I lived. I had been going there almost every day for about a year, and the owner would often cash me out. I was friendly with everyone, so I would smile at him and always thank him. One day, this man began to speak to me casually as he handed me my change. He said, "It's funny that I see you here almost every day and I don't even know your name." Oh, this wasn't for lack of noticing him. I had lived my life very guardedly, often putting up invisible walls until I got a good feel for someone, or let them know anything about me. Apparently, this facade either intrigued people or intimidated them. Some even took me for a snob, and I hadn't even realized this was how I came off.

The man from the diner introduced himself as Jim. He then asked me if I had time to sit down and have a quick coffee with him. *Wow*, I thought. This beautiful Adonis of a man actually wanted to have coffee with me. I nonchalantly agreed to sit down for a few minutes, and we got to know one another. All the while, I still kept a bit of my wall up, as he was so incredibly handsome and debonair that I could just tell he could have had any woman he chose. I played it very cool, careful not to portray myself as a woman who was entranced by his beauty. I didn't want to be categorized as just another conquest for this sort of man. Nonetheless, my heart was definitely pounding as I looked at him. He was well over six feet tall, with a physique like a marble statue. He was always dressed impeccably, and his Mediterranean skin had a bronzed glow. At thirty years old, his hair had already reached the salt-and-pepper stage. He had beautiful, deep-green eyes, and eyelashes that any woman would die for. Those attributes, along with his smile, were enough to warm the sternest of hearts.

The coffee turned into many coffees as the minutes turned into two hours. He told me he had wanted to talk to me for a very long time, but I had come off as being unapproachable and he didn't know how to break the ice. He also admitted while laughing that, because he never even knew my name, he had chosen the name P.J. for me because I smoked Peter Jackson cigarettes. He was Greek and quite fascinated by my young independence, but he was also very forthcoming about his marital status.

Jim came from a very prominent family that still abided by old-school rules. He told me that his marriage had been arranged back in Corfu when he was still a young boy. I had known he must have been married, and judging by his style and story, I was convinced there had to be other women in his life. Sure, he was charming and attractive, but I found no harm in being friends with him, as I had quite a few male friends and I loved chatting with him. The days passed, and many more coffees were shared between us.

One day, Jim asked me if he could take me out for dinner. I found it so exciting that this hunk of a man was asking me out for an evening. We went out, and I had what I felt to be the most romantic date of my life. He was a perfect gentleman. We drank good wine and ate at a beautiful restaurant. We even had a dance, which sent shivers up my spine. There were no words spoken and no sexual contact, but as he embraced me and we looked into one another's eyes, I felt as though an electric current had run through my entire being. I could feel the electricity radiate within him as well. This was a whole new feeling for me, but I certainly had no intentions of telling him that. All I knew was that my friendship was starting to feel more like something else.

Then and there, the thought hit me: This could quite possibly become my second affair with a married man. I was young and had never thought anything of it besides acknowledging that it was exciting and safe. I was actually more concerned with the fact that I was already crazy about this man, and I was determined not to let it show. I was quite wise when it came to men, as I'd had a lot of practice watching my mother control the male psyche, but I also knew that Jim had his share of women swooning after him, and I didn't intend to be just another statistic in his address book.

Jim and I went on quite a few dates before I ever invited him up to my apartment. I was very proud, and I never wanted to be anyone's one-night stand. From the first time we made love, it was like nobody else existed in the world. Our passions for one another would unleash themselves breathlessly, time and time again. It was as though we couldn't get enough of each other, not only sexually, but mentally as well. The feelings we had for one another stimulated our bodies right through to our souls, though I never once uttered the word *love* or anything related to it. I never asked about our future nor spoke to him about his marital situation—I was exhilarated with our relationship just as it was. I was wined, dined, and loved, treated like a princess by the handsomest prince in the land, or so it felt. I was still living under the guise that I never wanted to be married, so this lifestyle couldn't have been more perfect.

A few glorious months went by. One night, after another wonderful evening out, Jim and I went back to my place, where our fabulous outings usually ended up. Jim was sitting on my couch as I poured us a drink, and I noticed a forlorn look on his beautiful face. I knew him so well by then that his eyes were like open windows to his soul when we were together. I sat down beside him and snuggled into his arms while the captivating aroma of his cologne filled my senses. I asked him what was wrong, and he took my hand, looked into my eyes, and said, "Did it ever occur to you that I may have fallen in love with you?"

I remember the scene as though it were yesterday. His words were branded on my heart. The music was playing softly in the background, the candles were lit, and there was no other light but a hint shining down the hall from the ajar bathroom door. I stoically looked at him with a big, innocent smile and said no, though I was lying through the depths of my core. I was head over heels crazy for him, but I was never going to tell him that. I showed him affection and enjoyed every moment we spent together, but no words of love were going to come out of my mouth and ruin what we had by scaring him away. I knew he was just as crazy about me, but I never expected to hear the *love* word enter into our relationship. How naive had I been to think things would never change?

After I replied no to Jim's question, Jim told me how he'd had many women in his life but had made it a policy to never get involved too deeply. He had never wanted anything heavy to develop, because there could be no future for it, not with his marital status. This had become a problem for him because he had broken his own rule by falling in love with me. He told me there had been times when he had called his wife by my name accidentally, and he divulged his biggest concern about our relationship: He knew he could never get divorced, and he didn't feel as though he had the right to tie up my life. He was a possessive man, and he told me he didn't like it when I went out socially without him, though in the same breath, he added that he had no right to demand such a thing from me. He was brutally honest. He never made any far-fetched promises, and I was just content to be where I was with him. I had no desire to bring up unpleasant realities about our life and what it could be. We talked into the wee hours of the night and still made passionate love.

A few weeks later, we were once again out for dinner. Jim became quite sullen—lost in thought, it seemed. His mind was going in so many different directions. When I looked right into his eyes, I could see that our relationship had been taking its emotional toll on him ever since that night, when love had been mentioned. I was also feeling so many mixed emotions, and I constantly replayed that night over and over in my head. I was also careful not to say anything about love to him, not anymore. I think I felt safe knowing that if something happened to break us up, not telling him I loved him would make it easier on me.

My eyes reverted back to Jim as I snapped back to reality, and I suddenly found myself saying, "Jim, you look so sad. Is this relationship becoming too much of a burden for you? Would you feel better if we ended it?" Yes, though I appeared to remain calm, I could feel my heart race to my throat, while my hands nervously clenched the napkin on my lap. I was the brave soldier. I had blatantly asked him what I felt he so desperately wanted to say but couldn't find the words for. Stupidly, I had never, ever believed he would say yes. In that instant, the world stood still for me. I was so taken aback that I hadn't realized until that exact moment how much I loved him. I had truly just learned what a breaking heart felt like.

Jim began to explain his decision. "I can't do this anymore," he said. "I have no rights over you. I want you all the time, not part time, and that can never be." He told me we would always be friends and that he would always be there for me whenever I needed him, and he meant it. I had opened the door for him to admit what he had been agonizing over, but in the process I had been smacked by the door. By then, I could feel the tears welling up inside me, and I decided I couldn't sit through dinner. I asked Jim to walk me to my car, as I had met him there after work. I remember that night so vividly, as that was the night I learned a hard lesson in love.

It was like a scene out of *Romeo and Juliet*. Jim walked me to my car and grabbed me so tight. He held my face with his strong hands and looked me straight in the eyes. With tears streaming down his cheeks, he said, "I love you, P.J., like I've never loved any other and never will." As if that wasn't enough to break what was left of my heart, we kissed passionately. I pulled away for a second and looked him square in the eye, and I told him that I loved him so much and needed him to know that.

Jim and I did remain friends. Strangely enough, we picked up our friendship only days later. It didn't feel like anything had changed. He picked me up, and we went out for dinner, and, not surprisingly, we ended up back at my apartment, making torrid love. This made me happy, but I soon realized it wasn't ideal. When the night ended, it became awkward for both of us, yet we continued to see each other for a few more months. I began to feel Jim's inner torment surface, as we had gone back to where we started. We were like an addiction for one another.

Eventually, I called the play again. I had somehow become the spokesman for Jim's soul. I was a realist, and as much as I would have done anything not to lose him, I couldn't stand to see him in such anguish, so I unselfishly set him free. We were once again out for dinner, and by then, Jim's beautiful green eyes, which were always so intently focused on my every word, seemed only to be looking down at the table. Instinctively, I said, "Jim, you can't even look me in the eye anymore."

It hurt too much. We mutually decided that we would become faraway friends. This was the term I coined for us. Our emotions were like open wounds and needed time to heal before we could really go from lovers to friends, and it became very difficult for me to go to his diner to buy cigarettes. Eventually, I found a new place to get my smokes. This helped to lessen the pain. On the rare occasion I did go there, maybe once every few months, just to see his face and know that he was okay, all the memories would come flooding back in a single glance. It was as though no words were necessary. We knew what the other was saying and feeling just by looking at one another.

There were still lapses. Twice in that year, with just a glance, the electricity between us became almost visible. I just knew. I dashed home, and within a half an hour he would show up at my door and we would once again make passionate, desperate love as though no time had passed. But there were no words. No small talk, no talking about feelings, only our bodies communicating everything we couldn't say. Those were to be the last two times we would ever make love.

I grew a lot from those two action-packed years in my life. I learned undying love and real heartache. I also couldn't help but wonder: if I hadn't given Jim the opportunity to admit his unrest, or if I had responded to it by telling him I didn't care if he never left his wife, that it was my decision to be tied up with him, would we have remained together? I also discovered that there was a lot of harm in being with a married man. Besides the pain Jim caused by betraying his wife, I had never anticipated this sort of relationship could harm me, because I wasn't looking to get married. I had never entertained the thought that I could fall in love so hard it would actually hurt. Married men were no longer a safety feature for me. Jim would be the last of my adventures.

Coke, Love, and Cigarettes

I watched the years of heartache tug away at my dad, and it seemed that with every passing year, another piece of his heart was torn from him. Over time, I could see the light in his eyes grow just a little dimmer, as though all he had ever hoped for had disappeared and the will to fight for what he wanted out of life became secondary to simply existing.

I was still having weekly dinners with Dad, and I was still the apple of his eye. He took full bragging rights for anything I accomplished in life and supported all my ambitions, no matter how many times I changed my career path. He would cheer me on instead of chastising me for not being able to make up my mind. He was really proud of my achievements and how far I'd come from my shattered childhood, and he was happy I had made good friends. But Dad wasn't a healthy man, and I always worried about him. My maternal instincts didn't seem to disappear just because I had left home.

I had no ambitions to be a doctor, but I always tried to find a cure when I or someone I loved wasn't well. Besides the heartbreaks my father had endured over and over in his life, his habits were adding to his declining health. My dad just didn't seem to have any *joie de vivre* left in him. His children were his happiness, and he and I were very close, but he never remarried or seemed to get over losing my mother, and his sadness had manifested in his lifestyle. He didn't care how much garbage food he ate, and he smoked a pack of cigarettes a day. His real addiction was Coca-Cola, and he would drink many of those on a daily basis. He had a terrible fear of doctors, but I took the reins.

I hated seeing him let himself go down the path of self-destruction. I didn't even believe he was aware of what he was doing to himself. I knew it wasn't intentional; he just didn't want to change. I arranged, with my grandfather, to take my father to the Mayo Clinic in Rochester, Minnesota. I knew my father had been diagnosed with high cholesterol after his stroke of more than a decade past, and though he wouldn't listen to doctors, he seemed to listen to me. I thought that taking him to the Mayo Clinic would mean he could get completely checked out, and I could be there for the results and then try to make a healthy living plan for him to follow.

The Mayo Clinic was a magnificent, huge building complex with several underground tunnels leading to adjoining buildings. The waiting areas were like gymnasium-sized rooms. When we went to the clinic, Dad was put through rigorous testing of his heart and all his vitals. He was finally diagnosed with terribly high cholesterol levels and was told by the doctors that if he didn't change his lifestyle habits, he would eventually suffer a fatal heart attack. This was terrifying, but I found it amazing that by just changing his diet and eating healthy, he could bring down the bad levels and have a chance to live longer in good health.

I discussed dietary planning and all the other advice from the doctors with my father, and I promised him I would make him healthy as long as he promised to follow the plan with my help. I was so relieved to finally learn what was going on with him and get started on correcting the problem. I was also elated to get out of Rochester, as we were there in the dead of January and nothing could have prepared me for the depth of the cold and the amount of snow we encountered there.

When we returned, I shared the information with my sister, and we made plans to cook healthy meals weekly for Dad and take them to his apartment to keep in the freezer so he would always have something home-cooked to eat. I hated that he ate junk food off the lunch truck that passed by his work every day, downed with a couple of Cokes. For dinner, he'd always order pizza or Chinese food. I hounded him repeatedly about what he was eating, and sometimes he really tried to be good, but it seemed he would always revert back to his old ways despite all of our efforts. It seemed that these habits were really his comforts, and he just couldn't comprehend that something as simple as food could actually kill him.

Hospitality and Health

When I was twenty-five, I decided I wanted to work in the hospitality industry. I wasn't quite sure just how I could take the leap and find a position without any background experience, but I crafted a plan and struck it lucky. I had spent countless weeks looking through want ads, but it seemed none of the jobs appealed to me, and I didn't have the right requirements for those that did. I decided to take matters into my own hands and put together a great little résumé. I had retail experience and people skills, and I was an excellent typist, so surely I could find something interesting.

I called around to several hotels and began sending out my résumés randomly. As luck would have it, I got a call about a week later to interview for a position as an executive secretary to the general manager of the Ritz-Carlton Hotel. I was over the moon. In those days, it was all about the personal interview. It seemed any job I went after, I got.

It didn't take me long to get a grasp on the word processor, and the fact that my typing speed was ninety words per minute had to have been an asset. Oh, how I loved those days and that job! It was prestigious, and I loved the fact that I could get dressed up every day for work. The years of working in the fashion business—and my newly acquired beauty skills, thanks to my pal Zandra—had helped me develop a real flair for putting myself together. My job was stimulating, and I loved office organization and planning and deadlines. It also didn't hurt that I had a nice boss who was also very handsome. My enthusiasm and productivity never went overlooked, and within a year I had earned a substantial raise. For a girl in my position back in 1984, making $28K annually was pretty sweet.

One day, as I was getting ready for work, while putting on my makeup, a strange wave of doom flashed through me. I sat for a moment, trying to figure out what I was feeling, and then suddenly the phone rang. It was my sister, calling to let me know that my father had just suffered a heart attack. Initially, I froze. When I had composed myself, I darted straight off to the hospital. I thanked God for letting my dad survive, but the tests showed that his coronary arteries were very blocked. I remember being with him and the doctors, waiting to take him for an angiogram, and they were talking about putting a stent in to open up the arteries.

He would have no part in it—my father was petrified of doctors, hospitals, and needles. We all tried hard to make him understand the necessity of having this test and procedure, but he wouldn't budge. He eventually came home, and my sister and I tried to look after him as best we could. It was difficult to be with him a lot, as we both had jobs and I lived a good half hour away, but life went on, and my dad was back to work within a couple of weeks. I constantly worried for him, and the feeling was like a dark cloud that loomed inside me and never seemed to settle.

Greece

I loved to travel. My imagination had always taken me to beautiful places, and I would dream about countries I had never visited and picture how exotic and exciting they were. I was independent and fearless. At twenty-six, I had already done a bit of traveling, having been to Europe, parts of the United States, and various parts of Mexico and Venezuela. I had never been to Greece, however, and I had a great urge to visit the Greek islands. When I got an idea in my head, it very rarely disappeared until I could bring it to fruition.

I was still working at the hotel, but I couldn't shake my desire to take some time off and go to Greece. I didn't need anyone to accompany me, because I would often do things on my own, at my own pace, and I had never felt lonely. I was a very friendly, personable girl who had no problem attracting friends, and I had street smarts and good instincts that cautioned me to my surroundings.

I thought about taking the adventure for quite a while, but there were a few things I had to work out to make it happen. First, I needed some financial aid, and second, I didn't want to lose my job. I devised a great plan: I spoke with my dad and asked him if he would help me out financially to go on the trip. I let him know how much it meant to me and reminded him of the fact that I wasn't married, so this was the time for me to see the world. I also reminded him that it would have cost him a lot more to pay for my wedding than to send me on this trip! I was able to logically explain my thinking, and I had always been pretty crafty with words. My father couldn't refuse me, as he had always supported my dreams and admired my tenacity.

After I got the commitment from Dad, I had to come up with a plan to secure my job. What I devised was brilliant: Bri was in between jobs at the time, and I asked if she'd like to cover for me at work for a few months if I took a leave of absence. Bri was also a very personable girl, and anyone who knew her couldn't help but like her. She had also been very good at her past jobs as a bookkeeper and in office management. Bri wasn't just a friendly fill-in for my job—she was more than qualified. She said she would be thrilled to take on the work. I had grown quite excited by that time, as the prospect of the trip was looking good. I only had to speak with my boss to request the time off. Since I had found the perfect substitute for my position and wouldn't be leaving him in the lurch—not to mention that my job would be waiting for me when I came back—it was a win–win.

I made travel plans. I would be flying to Athens and had booked a small villa by the sea in Mykonos for two months. I thought this would be a good home base that would allow me to take little jaunts to other islands. There wouldn't be any backpacking for me, as I was a packrat and had way too much luggage. My friends got a hoot out of how much stuff I had to take with me every time I traveled: too many clothes and shoes, and half a bathroom full of toiletries.

I can say with certainty that traveling alone in a country like Greece in the mid eighties was hard enough as a single young girl without factoring in the three suitcases I had to tote with me along the way. As well, anyone who knew me back then knew very well that high-heeled shoes were like appendages for me. It didn't seem to matter the occasion, whether dancing or camping (which only happened once . . . and was a bad idea), I only ever wore heels. I didn't even own a pair of runners.

Arriving in Athens was like culture shock to me. The first thing that shocked me was the air pollution. As I rode in the taxi from the airport to the hotel, I could see exhaust seeping from many small vehicles on the crowded narrow roads. The air was thick and black as we drove. And so my journey had begun.

I would be staying in Athens for three days before heading to Mykonos to take over the villa rental. I went for walks to take in some sights, such as the Acropolis, and I would go to the market to pick up some healthier fare to eat. Although I wasn't yet eating a gluten-free diet at that time, I was still a picky eater, and I would usually get a fresh baguette, some feta cheese, and some beautifully ripe tomatoes. One night, I went to eat at an outside cafe to take in some city life. I ordered moussaka, which seemed to be floating in grease. I noted to myself that perhaps the country had been named for the amount of oil that seemed to drown everything I ate. I also became aware that I stood out like a sore thumb, sitting by myself amongst mostly men. With my platinum-blonde hair, which had become almost white in the blazing Mediterranean sun, I became very self-conscious about how touristy I appeared. It was an uncomfortable feeling, and I often felt like I was looked upon as easy prey while in Greece.

During my stay at the hotel, I met some fellow travelers. In particular, I met four people. First I met a married man holidaying there with his family, though it appeared to me as though he spent little time with them. His name was Eduardo, and he was from Verona, Italy. It seemed that any time I wandered through the hotel or went up to the pool, Eduardo would appear. It was as though he had radar on me. We talked about many things in those few short days, and I enjoyed his company. It was nice to have someone to talk to. He was quite a handsome man: tall and strong, with very fair hair, and he sported a goatee. When he looked at me, it was as though I could see stars in his eyes, as though he had been mysteriously captivated by me.

I also met a very nice Dutch boy named Iroen—pronounced *Ee-run*. I refer to him as a boy because he had a certain innocence to him, and he was probably a good five to six years younger than I was. Iroen was backpacking through Europe that summer on a limited budget, and our friendship grew fast. I had given him the address to where I would be staying in Mykonos and offered him one of the four bedrooms for a nominal fee if he passed through that island and found himself needing a comfortable place to stay. He happily placed the card in his wallet and thanked me for the offer. I also befriended a lovely young couple from Australia. They were also backpacking through Europe, and I extended the same invitation to them as I had to Iroen.

When the day came for me to leave Athens and take the ferry to Mykonos, I said good-bye to all my new friends and wished them all safe travels. When Eduardo came to say goodbye to me, he cornered me in the hotel corridor and gave me a big hug. In a split second, his hug turned into a passionate kiss, and he looked into my eyes and told me he loved me. As startling as I found his sudden kiss, I found it more bizarre and slightly amusing that this man could tell me he loved me after knowing me for only three days and with a language barrier between us. I suppose Italian men were known as romantics because of incidents like this. He handed me a note with an address and phone number where he could be reached. I was flabbergasted. I had figured he had those kinds of feelings for me, although telling me he loved me seemed a bit much. Even though the kiss had been so unexpected, it made me feel beautiful. That was the last contact I ever had with Eduardo.

Getting on that ferry with too many suitcases was no small feat. Ironically, no chivalrous men stepped up to give me a hand getting my bags on the ship. Finally, the porter came down some steps to lift my exceedingly heavy suitcases aboard, but not without grunting about how heavy they were and asking me why I needed so many bags. It wasn't funny to me then, but he was definitely right.

I finally arrived in Mykonos the next day after one stormy, seasick sail. As I gathered my things and waited for a taxi to take me to the villa, I stood in wonder at my surroundings. The view of the Aegean Sea was picturesque, with its rippling turquoise and multiple shades of blue. When I looked at the town ahead, past the pier, I felt as though I were looking at something out of a fairy tale. There were cobblestone paths that seemed to lead in one hundred different directions, like a maze, and the small stores along the streets linked to one another, basic cement with barred windows and a door. All the buildings and homes were painted blue and white, as was the custom of the island.

I finally flagged a taxi, and the driver struggled to load my worldly possessions into the trunk. I welcomed the shelter from the sweltering August heat. It was only a short drive straight up a narrow, dusty road to the villa, though saying the road went up is an understatement. This road had quite an incline, and I kept praying under my breath that the old taxi would be able to make it up the hill.

When we arrived, there was an old woman standing outside a tiny house at the bottom of a steep hill, waiting to greet me. She wore a blue kerchief on her head, and stood hunched over on her cane. She spoke hardly a word of English as she pointed up to the top of the steep hill. I was looking at my villa. From my vantage point, it seemed the house sat atop a small mountain, with many broken steps and intermittent weedy terrain leading upward. I immediately thought that just coming in and out of the house would be great exercise, and I was grateful to have two good legs. I presumed this woman was the keeper of the keys for whoever owned the rather big house. I was thankful that the taxi driver carried my bags up the steep hill, and I once again reprimanded myself for bringing so damn much luggage.

When we went inside, the old woman mimed me a tour. The house was quite large, with four bedrooms, two bathrooms, and a kitchen. The furniture was minimal and quite rustic, there was nothing on the walls, and all the floors were cold and made of marble. The kitchen had a gas stove, which scared me because it was so foreign. The woman gave me a quick demonstration of how to turn it on by lighting it with a match, and though this scared the shit out of me, I supposed I would have to get used to it if I wanted to eat. I felt as though I had moved into some ancient place and time.

After I settled in, I went to take a look at the beach. The walk down the dangerously steep hill from the house seemed to take longer than the rest of the walk to the beach, about one hundred meters from the bottom of the hill. The water sparkled with its varying degrees of blue. I was located on a serene little area of the island, and I decided to head back into town to stock up on some groceries, as it appeared there was only one tiny beach cafe in the vicinity. I was grateful that a bus ran straight up and down that dusty road every half hour from town to the beach and back. It was starting to feel like I was living a real adventure.

When I got into town, I decided to wander and take a look around before I was saddled with carrying groceries. One could get lost so easily, as it was a crapshoot as to which path I would choose from the myriad cobblestone streets. As destiny would have it, I found myself staring through the window into a jewelry store—this happened to be another one of my weaknesses. Being obsessed with jewelry, I was sure I wanted to buy a small token as a remembrance of my trip. I entered the store and purchased a small filigree silver band with the Greek key embossed around it.

The man in the store was quite charming. He was the cliché of tall, dark, and handsome, though one could almost see the devil in his eyes. He was friendly and very chatty, and he introduced himself as Theo. He seemed to be fascinated that a young, blonde, American girl—this was the assumption of everyone I encountered—was by herself in his store. He looked at me with piercing, dark eyes and asked me how long and where I would be staying. I was very cautious and had made it a policy to never divulge to strangers that I was traveling alone or where I was staying, as I was leery and had to get a good sense of someone before I gave away any personal details. I thanked him for his assistance and told him it had been nice to make his acquaintance. Then I went on my way to get my groceries and headed back to my villa.

A couple of weeks passed, and I was getting used to the tranquil surroundings. I went to the beach daily and caught up on lots of reading, as there was a clever little alcove set up on the beach as a makeshift bookstand, full of books people had read, kind of like a trade-in booth. When someone was done reading a book, they would leave it there for somebody else to enjoy, and they were free to take any other book in return. It was a great idea, most likely invented by tourists so there would always be something new to read.

I was starting to feel a bit restless. Though the days were beautiful and peaceful, the long nights alone at the top of the hill left me wanting something more. I didn't really know anybody, and I was terrified of going out alone at night. I had never even considered climbing that long, bumpy hill in the dark, and as it was pitch-black at night, I was not about to stand on that dusty road alone, waiting for a bus. It was time for me to make plans to visit some other islands. I decided that when the sun rose, I would trek into town and make arrangements.

The next morning, I took the bus to town in the hot, blazing sun. When I stepped off the rickety old bus, there was a very steep drop, and as I stepped onto the broken cement sidewalk, my left foot turned inward as I landed on it. I heard the crack of my anklebone, and I instantly fell to the ground. It took me a few minutes to get up, and nobody offered any assistance. The pain was excruciating as I stood there on one foot in the scorching sun. I was in a terrible predicament, alone in a strange country with a broken foot. I stood for a few minutes with tears streaming down my cheeks before quickly getting myself into survival mode.

I began to think about where I could go to get help. I didn't know the island or even where the hospital was. Nobody seemed to care that I couldn't walk. I realized then that the only soul I knew was Theo, the man in the jewelry store. This option didn't thrill me, but it was my only way to find help. I hopped on one foot and followed the only path I was familiar with to the jewelry store. As I hopped along, I pressed my hand off and on the wall to propel me until I made it. Theo was there. He remembered me instantly and quickly offered me a chair. I asked him if he could tell me where I could find a doctor, and he graciously offered to take me through the maze of paths. There were no cars on that island, only taxis and buses, and most people got around on little motorbikes. The only way to get through those tiny streets, though, was by foot, so Theo carried me to the town's doctor.

The doctor told me my foot was broken. There was no hospital on the island, so I would have to go by boat to the next island, Syros, which had a hospital, in order to get a cast. I remember that day clear as a bell because it was one of those days where I thought it couldn't get any worse, and then it did. The doctor told me all he could do was wrap my foot and ankle tightly in a tensor bandage and give me crutches. I made my decision right then—there was no way I was going by boat to some Stone Age hospital.

"So, let me ask you this," I said. "If I let you wrap it and I use crutches and keep my foot up as much as possible without putting any weight on it, will it heal?"

He told me it would, eventually, but it most likely wouldn't heal properly.

"Are you telling me that if I leave here on crutches and take the best care that I can of my foot, it will eventually mend and the worst that can happen when I return home is that I may have to have it broken and reset?" I asked.

He said yes.

I was elated. I immediately replied, "That's a chance I'm willing to take."

I'll just say that the island was hard enough to walk on with two good legs, let alone with crutches. Theo felt very sorry for me, but as much as I needed and appreciated his help, I couldn't help but feel uneasy when he was around me. The way he looked at me made me very uncomfortable, and in that situation I was vulnerable. However, I needed his support.

Theo insisted on taking me back to my villa. As much as I didn't want him to know where I was staying, I had no choice. There was no way I could have made it up the hill back to my villa. I agreed to let him take me home. He carried me back to the harbor, where we could wait for a taxi. The harbor was chaotic, as a ship had just recently docked, and there was a shortage of taxis. We waited for more than an hour in that sweltering heat before finally getting a cab.

It was barely a two-mile ride up the dusty road, but the taxi's transmission died halfway, so we had to get out and hope for another one to pass. What seemed like another hour went by before a man rode by on a beat-up, three-seater motorbike. Theo asked him if he would take us the other mile up the road, and he did. I really didn't think the bike would make it up the hill with the three of us and a pair of crutches—you can't even make this shit up!

When we finally arrived, Theo gave the man some money and carried me and my crutches up the rickety, steep path before putting me down at the door. I thanked him for all he had done for me, but he insisted on helping me inside and said he needed a glass of water. I couldn't deny him water after all he had gone through for me in the stifling heat.

When we got inside, I was not only worn out from the exhausting venture and drained from the heat, but the throbbing in my foot had yet to let up. I hopped into the kitchen to get us some water. Before I could do anything, Theo gently took both his and my water glasses and rested them on the nicked wooden table in the hallway where he stood. He then put his arms around me and pulled me close. All I could think at that moment was *Oh my God, does this day get any worse?* I thought he was going to rape me. He tried to kiss me, and I pulled back. He was quite handsome, with his toned physique and his dark, Mediterranean features, but something about him left me with a very unsettled, creepy feeling.

I felt like I had to think quickly. I wanted to remain calm and polite, as I didn't want to make him angry or make him feel like I was rejecting him or his generosity—but there was no way I owed him any sexual favor in gratitude. He told me how attracted he had been to me since we first met, and I babbled on, trying to keep the conversation going to dissuade what I felt were his real intentions. Then I blatantly said, "Have I not been through enough today? I'm feeling lots of pain, and I need to go to sleep."

After what seemed an eternity of hoping God would hear my silent prayers to make this man leave, he replied, "Okay, you look like you need to rest. I'll go back to work, and when I close my shop tonight, I'll come back and check on you."

Those words petrified me. I thanked him for everything he had done for me and gave him an unemotional hug, and he left. At that point, all I felt was an overwhelming fear of nightfall. There was no way I was going to let this guy back inside. I was scared of being in a desolate location on top of the dark hill by myself. I quickly put my crutches down and began hopping around, moving furniture to block the door in preparation for nightfall. At dusk, I closed all the windows and shutters and kept a knife close by my side. My heart raced as I lay for long hours, waiting for that long night to pass. He never came.

I hibernated in my fortress for another whole day and night. By the following day, I was going stir crazy between my scary thoughts and my antsy boredom starting to set in. I hadn't been able to make any travel arrangements due to the circumstances, and the possibility of that happening now was nil. I couldn't travel alone on crutches with three suitcases and no assistance. I decided it was time to at least go back to the beach. I needed sunshine and the sound of people around me.

*

It was a long, careful trek down the steep hill on my crutches with my beach bag in tow. The five-minute walk on the uneven, dusty road to the beach had taken its toll on my armpits, and when I finally got to my spot on the sand, I crawled and picked up a big rock to position under my leg so I could lie down and keep my foot elevated. About an hour passed as I happily lazed in the sun before God sent me an angel.

I thought I heard someone calling my name from a distance. At first, I thought I was hallucinating, and I wondered if I had just taken in too much sun or Tylenol. But I wasn't hallucinating. I looked up, and from about twenty feet away I saw my little Dutch friend, Iroen, coming toward me. I couldn't remember ever having been so excited to see someone. Iroen had kept my address, and being that he was on a limited budget and had mostly been staying in youth hostels, he had decided to come visit and stay somewhere nice for a treat. That was when I realized that we truly meet people for a reason—if only for a season!

Iroen stayed with me for almost three weeks. We became close friends, and it was a godsend to have him around. He carried my things when we went to the beach, cooked us many dinners, and we took several trips to town together. Life had become fun once again. I had a companion and lots of help. There was nothing sexual between us, for Iroen had become like a brother to me. We talked about everything, comparing our lives and our respective countries and cultures. We would keep in touch by letter for many years after.

Eventually, our time together came to an end. He was ready to move on to another island and had already stayed much longer than planned. We said our good-byes at the beach, as Iroen had taken me there for the last time before he left. I never took a dime of rent from him.

I've always felt that if you believe in miracles, you believe they can happen more than once. Iroen had departed, and as I lay on the beach, I began thinking that since I was on my own again, I should just cut the vacation short and make plans to go home. However, before that day ended, I heard someone calling my name. Actually, it was two voices I heard. In disbelief, I saw my Aussie friends, Andy and Rayna. I couldn't believe my blessed luck. They were still touring the Greek islands and were also on a limited budget, so they were quite happy to take me up on my invitation.

They stayed with me for two weeks and helped me every-where we went. We took in a lot of sights, as it was easy for me to do things again with assistance. Every afternoon, we had a ritual where Rayna would make us tea. She would always say she was going to make us a "cuppa," just one of the many Aussie terms she used, and I found this so amusing that I nicknamed them my cuppa friends. I was so happy to have befriended them.

Alas, our time together came to an end. Andy and Rayna were moving on to the next country, as they were planning on touring Europe, backpacking for a year and picking up odd jobs along the way to supplement their travel costs. Staying with me for two weeks had been a cozy holiday for them, and I hadn't asked them to pay rent as they had been so kind and helpful, including me in all their activities.

By then, just over two months had gone by. I decided that I had been away long enough. I had traded up the crutches for a cane, which the old woman down the hill had given to me. My leg was still bandaged tight daily, only now it was just to my calf instead of my knee. I was now limping on it gently as I went into town once again to make travel arrangements. I called my dad to tell him I was ready to come home, and I cried my eyes out at the comforting sound of his voice. I was homesick. It was time to go home.

Aunty Sherry

Not many months after I returned from Greece, I received a phone call from my mother: Aunty Sherry had cancer. At that point in time, my aunt was no longer working, as the rental office had been closed down for over a year because the buildings were at full occupancy. This no longer mattered to her, though, as she was still mourning the loss of her beloved husband. Two years before, Uncle Neil had suddenly been stricken with a fatal heart attack. God had taken the love of her life from her, and as though that wasn't punishment enough, she herself was now suffering from the dreaded cancer. It all made me wonder why such a jubilant woman, so full of life, had been made to suffer two devastating events, but I have since learned not to question God's plans.

I was sickened to the core of my being. My world was certainly rocked. My aunt was a brave warrior—she took her licks in stride and never gave up. She also had a phobia of doctors, just like my father did. I was told she had pancreatic cancer, though I was never given the intimate details as to how this suddenly seemed to come about. The truth is that I'm quite certain it wasn't sudden. I know she had suffered lots of gynecological problems and had refused to see a doctor, and based on facts I had gathered here and there, I surmised her disease may have progressed and spread from one of her reproductive parts.

Cancer has always been a horrifying, devastating word, back in the eighties and in the present. The only difference was that, back then, it wasn't common to hear about it. All I knew was that my maternal grandfather had died from it. Whenever I went to visit her, she was still the same Aunty Sherry. She held her head high and managed to smile, never showing anything but courage. We chose not to speak about her battle. Our visits were just like old times, only I was now carrying extra sorrow in my heart. We would sit on her old couch in the little apartment where she shared her life with her beloved husband for just over a decade, and I would fill her in on my exciting adventures, which she was always so interested in. If there was a baseball game, she would turn it on, as the only passion left in her life was for the Toronto Blue Jays, of whom she was a fanatical fan.

A couple years later, she was getting much worse, even after going through treatments. By that time, she had grown the most horrific tumor outside her body, between her breasts. It was literally the size of a five-pin bowling ball and just as black. It horrified me that this could happen to a human being. I could never seem to get any answers when I asked why it couldn't be removed—and this was just another of my many questions that never seemed to be explained. All I was told was that my aunt's case was going to be published in some medical journal because it was such a strange phenomenon.

As time went by, our visits became more and more solemn. She was finding it difficult to eat, and the laughter was gone from her voice and her eyes. She was in stage four pancreatic cancer. I went to visit her as often as I could, and I refused to acknowledge that she wouldn't somehow get better, although all signs led to the inevitable. She had become very weak and very ill, and as stubborn as she was, she was adamant about wanting to be sick at home and not in a hospital. As much as she never talked about death, she had blatantly said that she would not die in a hospital.

*

One autumn morning in 1989, my phone rang at around four. It was my mother at the hospital with my aunt. She told me to come right away, as my aunty didn't have long to live. I dressed as quickly as I could and dashed off to the hospital. When I arrived, my mother was sitting beside my aunt on her hospital bed, holding her hand. She was gone.

I cried my heart out to the depths of my soul. I got on the bed and lay beside her, comforting her lifeless body as though she was still with us. I don't recall how much time passed before my mother eventually told me I had to get up, as it was time for my aunt to be taken away. My heart ached so badly that I felt as though it had been shattered into pieces. That was the most pain I had ever experienced. I felt as though I had lost my mother.

*

Through all the years, hardly a day has gone by that I don't miss her or talk about her as though it was only yesterday that she was here. She didn't have many worldly possessions, for she wasn't a materialistic person. She had a simple gold wedding band that was left to me, which I still wear to this day. She is branded in my heart, and I feel her spirit around me. Sometimes, she comes to me in the echoed scent of perfume, and I take comfort in her memory.

Aunty Sherry, I love you.

Leaving the Hotel

About a year after my return from Greece, I learned about making big decisions and taking a risk on money versus security.

One day at work, as I was happily typing away, I received a phone call. A family friend, Stan, who had become a personal friend of mine, was calling to ask if we could meet for a coffee later that day. He said he wanted to talk to me about a business proposition. Stan was a sweet guy who had a heart of gold, but it seemed he'd never had much luck in past businesses. Most of that bad luck was due to him continually going into partnership with people who took advantage of his good nature. We met up for coffee, and he had brought with him a friend, Sal. Apparently, Sal was a builder, and Stan had invested with him as a partner. They had opened a new construction company and were coming to me with an offer.

Stan wanted me to run the office for him and oversee the company finances, taking charge of organizing the trades by scheduling and inspecting deficiencies. The money offered was attractive to me, and so was the offer of a brand-new company car. I thought long and hard about giving up my great position at the hotel, which was pretty much secure, with room for possible advancement, but I eventually accepted Stan's offer. I looked at it as a new venture in a cozy position with lots of added perks. Hindsight would have been twenty–twenty if I had really thought about the future, but being younger doesn't afford one those kinds of smarts.

The job was fabulous for the first year. I found it challenging, and it certainly expanded my dating circle. But as time went by, the finances seemed to be getting out of control. Sal really didn't have a handle on how to price jobs correctly, which meant Stan had to continually fork out cash into the company. Sal was a smooth-talking bullshitter, and I could see right through him. I tried many times to warn Stan that he was putting his cash into a losing proposition: The finances were upside down, and he was going to be drained of all his money eventually. It was my job to keep an eye on everything, including the books, and I felt it was also my responsibility to watch out for Stan, because it seemed his life pattern was repeating. Sal was taking advantage of Stan's good nature and trust. The company closed after only two years, and I was left jobless and carless.

After I licked my wounds from leaving the hotel, it wasn't long before I got another job. Another friend of mine owned his own public relations firm, and he was looking for a new office manager, so I happily accepted the offer. While working there, I met a man who was a freelance editor working on one of the firm's projects. This man sometimes came to the office for meetings, and after he asked me out, we continued seeing one another until our relationship became exclusive.

The relationship went on much longer than it should have. As the months turned into years, I learned just how unhealthy it was to keep this man in my life, but I had made some bad decisions along the way that kept me tied to him. I had become a victim. At first I unknowingly allowed it, but after much time passed, my self-esteem became so deflated that I just accepted it.

Dad

Illness: the result of letting something gnaw away at your core until it bores so deeply that you bleed out.

My father hated the cold. He loved Florida, Miami Beach in particular. When we were small, we had a condo there for a few years. Unfortunately, that condo only lasted as long as the latest reconciliation between my parents, barely two years, but my father still went to Florida every winter. He would always invite my sister and me, and later my sister's kids, to join him for however long we could get away, and he also always kindly paid for our airfare. I had gone there every year since moving away from home. For years we'd stayed at a local motel right on the beach, and it wasn't until some years later that he started renting a condo again.

I was thirty-one at the time, still in an unhealthy relationship, and I was also having some gynecological issues. The day was January 7, 1991, just after I had been diagnosed with early-stage cervical cancer. I had been home for about three hours after having a biopsy, and I was lying on the couch resting. Within the next few days, I would be heading off to Florida with my sister and her kids to stay with my dad. Late in the afternoon, my sister called me to see how I was feeling, and we chatted a bit about our plans for later that week. Throughout the call, her phone was beeping with the call waiting feature, so I hung on the line while she answered it. When she came back to our conversation, she wasn't the same sister I had been talking to only moments before.

Melanie was screaming in barely intelligible words. I struggled to make out what she was saying as I felt fear flood through my body. Then I heard her clearly. Her wailing sounded like something out of a horror movie. "Daddy is dead!" she finally managed to blurt out. I went into shock, dropping the receiver and leaving it dangling. I screamed with gut-wrenching sobs until there was no sound left in me, and then I lay on my couch, motionless, almost paralyzed. It was as though my soul had frozen over. My daddy had been taken from me.

It was a massive heart attack. He had been sitting in a chair in the condo, talking with a friend, and in what seemed an instant, he just keeled over onto the floor. Later, I would manage to thank God that he hadn't been alone.

Bri came by not long after I received the news to check up on me from my biopsy. She had a key, but she knocked, and I couldn't move to answer the door. She could hear my howling sobs from down the corridor, and she rushed in to find me in a state of hysteria. After trying to comfort me to no avail, she helped me put some clothes on so she could take me to my sister's house, where I would meet with my brothers to "make plans." There was no time to waste because we had to get our father home as quickly as possible for burial. Because my father had died in another country and our religion doesn't embalm, we had to expedite his body back to Canada as fast as the legalities would permit.

There were four of us. We all had a mission. Rory and Melanie had to fly to Miami to retrieve my father's body. They had to cut through a lot of red tape to get him home so quickly, but he was with us before the next day ended. Robby took care of the cemetery arrangements, and I got to go shopping—I went to the funeral home to buy my daddy a casket.

Dad was buried the next day, January 9, 1991. It's strange how we can't seem to remember many things from the past, yet we sometimes relive certain moments with such clarity. My father's passing is still vividly clear to me. Though I allow myself to relive it, the details never change. The ending stays the same, and my heart aches all over again.

Bees Find Honey

Throughout my twenties, I hadn't had a lot of contact with my mother. In fact, I had mostly seen her at clubs or at an occasional family celebration. I had never really shared my intimate life with my mother, as she had never asked me anything. Over time, I became selfish with the details of my life because of her lack of interest.

I had never really felt at ease around my mother, especially in situations where she could drink, when she would make things exceedingly uncomfortable for me or my siblings. I really did feel sorry for her when she drank too much, as it made her very melancholy and vulnerable. I hated those episodes and made every effort to stay clear of her. It seemed those were the times she would get touchy-feely, and I felt this was not at all genuine. However, I also believed those were the moments when she may have seen herself for how she really was and realized how lonely she was, with no real connection to anyone.

Some may say there is truth in wine, and I believe to some extent that this is true. When my mother would drink too much, her motto became, "Woe is me." I think she grew sad because certain truths may have surfaced in her subconscious, making her see herself clearly. Those were the moments when she would profess how much she loved us, and this made me quite uncomfortable. Perhaps I didn't believe her, or perhaps

I had felt so neglected by her all my life that I felt betrayed by this behavior, that it had only taken a few drinks for her to tell me. She would go on to say, "Don't you love me?" When she barely got a response, she would add, "Was I such a terrible mother?" I would feel guilty and appease her, but it never felt natural to me. It felt foreign to tell my mother I loved her.

Through the years of learning about my mother's many lies and exaggerations, I began to realize that when she made up stories to make herself stand out, she actually believed herself. She was a pathological liar who could lie point-blank to my face and stand adamant in her words, living in denial about anything she didn't want to acknowledge. She was certainly beyond my control, and I never wanted to be part of her lies. I had followed her antics for so long that I hated her for them, but I had also begun to feel sorry for her. She really needed help, but, sadly, she didn't think she had any flaws.

My dad had a small insurance policy that was left to his four children after he passed. When we received this money, we all got a phone call from our mother stating that she somehow felt entitled to some of it. Of course, none of us believed she deserved one red cent, but out of the goodness of our hearts, and mostly because none of us wanted to listen to her ranting if we denied her, we all chipped in and cut her a nice check.

My mother's jet-setting life and love of gambling continued. When we gave her that money, she took off for Florida to live on a girlfriend's houseboat for two years. During her absence, I never once spoke to her, though she called my sister every once in a while, asking about the grandkids and telling Melanie to say hello to me for her. When she had money, she disappeared, and as puzzling as I found it, I never missed her, as you can't really miss someone who has never been there.

She eventually hit my brothers up for money so she could remain in Florida, but they'd finally had enough. She had no choice but to come back to Toronto, and my siblings and I arranged a meeting with her to talk about getting some help.

We were hoping to end her delusions of grandeur, her fantasy life. When she returned from Florida, we all sat down with her at Robby's house and openly told her how we felt about the way she was living. My brothers told her they weren't going to support her life of leisure and luxury anymore when they were working to support their own families.

This hit a nerve with my mother. Any time one of us gave something to our own family members, she acted out in anger and jealousy. She would say, "I'm the mother. I always come first." I found it so absurd that she believed that just because she had given birth to us, we owed her a debt and her needs took precedence over everyone else's. This was part of her delusion. When I spoke, I had a question for her. I asked, "What kind of mother takes off for almost three years with her children's money and doesn't even call her daughter?" I also told her that as far as I was concerned, I was an orphan. I had no parents. She cried, admitting she needed help and promising she was going to change, but we all know the old saying: A leopard can't change its spots.

Taking My Lumps

I got involved in a relationship at a very uneventful time in my life. It appeared that after a decade of excitement, the tide was changing. I was getting a little older, and the nights of partying into the wee hours of the morning and going to work on limited sleep had worn out their welcome. It seemed my friends were now settling into their own lives. I continued to evaluate my life, and I began going through a self-questioning phase, asking, *Is this all there is?* I was quite independent and still had no desire to marry, and I struggled with the subject of whether I ever wanted children.

I thought about this a lot, as I heard my biological clock ticking, yet the thought of children wasn't appealing to me. If I ever wanted to have children, I had to start thinking seriously about it, yet I just couldn't picture myself as a mother. There was no particular reason for this, but I think I felt some deep-rooted fear stemming from my childhood, a feeling like I had already raised kids and didn't want to do it again. I battled those thoughts for years, and I sometimes worried I would have regrets down the road.

I still had a lot to learn about life, but at the time I believed that the fun years were behind me and that it was time to get serious in a relationship. I had dated many men, but I was so picky, finding fault in most of them as though I were searching for perfection. I was so confused. Did everyone find Mr. Right one magical day, or did there come a point where you just had to settle? Many people had told me that when the right one came along, I would just know it. I hadn't felt that way since Jim, and I was still carrying a torch for him. I really believed that finding the right person only happened in the movies, so romance became a gamble to me. Would I end up forever alone, or should I just stay in this relationship?

I had numerous conversations with Bri about my thoughts on relationships. The editor and I dated frequently, and I wasn't sure he was the guy for me no matter how crazy he was about me. My heart had never felt whole again after Jim and I parted ways, and I had resolved myself to thinking that nobody could ever replace him, that anyone else could only come second to Jim. I knew nobody could ever fill his shoes, so I assumed I had already gotten my great love and I should just go with whatever life brought me. Bri would often lecture me through our talks, telling me I was so hard on guys, that I didn't give them a chance. She kept telling me that I had found a nice guy and that he was good to me, that I should give the relationship a chance to grow, so I did. Still, there was something I just couldn't peg about him. I couldn't quite put my finger on it, but my sixth sense seemed to be raising some red flags.

A year into that relationship, I had given up my apartment, thinking it was time to grow up and move on to solidify the relationship. Nobody, including me, could believe I was going to give up my sanctuary after twelve years. I had lived a lifetime there, going through some of the happiest and saddest moments of my entire life. Bri helped me move out. The day I moved was a sad one for us both. Instead of feeling excitement about moving on to my new life, I was sad for the life I was leaving behind. Bri and I filled her car with the last load of my things and I turned my keys in to the superintendent. On the ride away from Roseview Circle, we both cried over the good times we had shared in my little apartment.

*

It didn't take more than a few days before I felt homeless, as though I were nothing more than an unwelcome guest. As our relationship progressed, I realized my suspicions didn't go unfounded. Unfortunately, until I realized my misjudgements, I subjected myself into the clutches of a demeaning, emotionally unbalanced person. While I endured many episodes of verbal and sometimes physical abuse, I had forgiven over and over because I felt it was my duty to help fix this person, not realizing the situation was beyond my aid. It was a very unhappy time for me as I felt I was walking on eggshells around this man, and anything I said could be twisted out of context and be followed with reprimanding me with ominous outbursts, accompanied by a pointed index finger to my face. As time passed, I grew more uncomfortable, worrying about what landmine I might set off next. I found myself always trying to appease him, to keep him happy. These sometimes alcohol-infused incidents seemed to be occurring more and more frequently. I had threatened to leave many times, though it seemed my compassion had succumbed to his heartfelt apologies over and over. After about a year of living under his tyranny, I decided it was time to move, time to get my own place. The real estate market was crashing fast and furious at the time, which made it an opportune moment for me to jump on the bandwagon and take advantage of becoming a first-time buyer.

By that time, I had gone back to school and taken a course to become a licensed croupier. Charity casinos had become a hot commodity at that time in Toronto, and I thought it would be a fun career for me, as I loved to play cards and the job was quite social. The money was good, and the tips were better.

In the weeks before I moved out, there were many apologies for his lousy treatment toward me. For some bizarre reason, I felt very bad for him . . . and I caved. Even though I had bought a condo and I was ready to move on, I again conceded to the apologies and once again tried to repair the relationship. I had thought because the tables had turned and he would now be living under my roof that things would change, and if they didn't, he would be the one having to leave... I hadn't learned. I don't know what led me to believe things would change, but being an optimist, I truly believed they would.

As the next year passed, I had two things keeping me sane. I had a great job, and my sister lived minutes away from me. She was a single mother at the time, and she was home every night with her children. Her girlfriends used to congregate there to keep her company, and often they would hold card games to pass the evening. That gave me a great place to go when I didn't want to be home.

I realized I had made numerous mistakes starting from the very beginning, when I had sensed some red flags yet continued with the relationship. By that time, I was living in fear of his spontaneous wrath. His moods were breaking my spirit, and I felt like I was constantly walking on edge around him. He would go off on a tangent for the most insignificant and ridiculous things, and it didn't take much to set him off, such as if the handle of the pot on the stove was facing outward.

After two years had passed, his belittling of me and everything I did had begun to take a toll on my self-esteem. I had lived this long with him on the assumption that those were the cards I had been dealt and I may as well just learn to deal with it. It was as though I had been brainwashed. My friends and family constantly nagged me, asking why I was staying with this emotionally unstable man. The berating was ongoing, and just as plentiful were the apologies the next day.

The worst part for me was wondering how I could finally sever the relationship without losing half of my condo in the process. After weighing various scenarios in my head for a breakup plan, I finally came to a decision. No matter how I envisioned asking him to leave, I didn't anticipate a smooth ending, so I decided to take the long road. The plan I came up with was the do-nothing approach, I didn't dare anger him, so I decided to use silence and not staying at home much in the hopes he would tire of me. I resolved myself to wait out the situation. I figured that if I continued to act in this way, he would realize we no longer had anything together and he would leave on his own accord, without a fight. The plan worked eventually, but not without it taking a toll on me for a good four more years of my life.

*

Going into the third year of the breakup plan, I was finally regaining my self-esteem. My social life was flourishing with a new circle of friends from work.

One day, he came home from work with welcome words. He told me he was going to find a place to live, since it was evident we had fallen apart. He said he had noticed I was going on with my life and had finally noticed our disconnect. I couldn't get over how many years it had taken for him to get the hint, but I was elated.

I had remained monogamous throughout our whole relationship even though I hadn't shared a bed with him for a few years. This wasn't out of loyalty to him but mostly out of fear. We were still living under the same roof, and I knew his erratic tendencies would surface if he ever discovered an indiscretion.

My job had expanded, and I had become a pit boss at work. I was also offered a job with a private company doing casino functions, mostly working on my own, dealing blackjack or poker. It was a great social job and kept me working a few nights a week. A lot of these events were stag parties, and there was never any shortage of male attention. I had received many dating invitations, although I never accepted any during that time.

It seemed like a long time until I was finally free again, and four years was a long time. There were many unpleasant incidents that occurred through those years, some last-ditch efforts on his part to try to repair or rekindle our relationship. On his final attempt to reconcile, just before he moved out, he threatened my life. It was by the grace of God that I had escaped. While I cannot go into details, it was not long after that incident that I was finally free.

I paid dearly. I sacrificed years, and my self-esteem, but I was no longer, or would I ever again, allow myself to be a victim. I danced like a teenager all through my home. I could breathe again. I felt new life running through my veins and a million pounds of weight being lifted off my soul. I had survived abuse.

Life Is a Circle

One night, when I was at work setting up the blackjack table in preparation for the evening's event, I just about swallowed my heart. It was a typical Friday night gig, and I was dealing cards at a groom's stag party in a banquet hall. The room was full of men, and I enjoyed chatting with everyone, as it was a friendly social environment and inter-action was the key to making good tips. While I was setting up the table, just as I was laying out a fresh deck of cards, I looked up and saw someone nearby. It was as though I had seen a ghost.

There, standing in front of me in all his handsome glory, was Jim. I got so nervous I thought I was going to throw up. My heart seemed to be racing at a million beats per minute. He smiled and said, "P.J.?" It seemed as though he had to question whether it was really me, and I remember being grateful that I had gotten all dolled up that night. It had become sort of a habit for me to make sure I always looked my best when going out, because I never knew who I might encounter. A girl never wants to be caught not looking her best when the man who still holds a piece of her heart might someday appear—and he had!

I supposed he said my name like a question because I had

since become a redhead, having been a natural blonde when he last saw me. I replied, "Jim?" Then we laughed and hugged one another. It had been almost a decade since I last saw him, but my heart felt as though it had only been yesterday. In a quick flash, I relived our relationship, and I still felt an aching loss for him as though the wound was fresh. The years had been kind to him: He was still as debonair and handsome as always, if not more, and he was still such a gentleman.

I had to get busy and open up the table, so he asked me to join his table for dinner so we could catch up. Dinner was my break time, when I normally chose a table and sat down with the guests. This gave me the opportunity to socialize and invite them to play cards after dinner. I felt the most exciting rush flow through my being, something I hadn't felt for years.

At dinner, we talked about our lives, and that half hour we spent talking felt like a lifetime, though it went by in a split second. There was a table full of men, but it was as though only Jim and I existed. When I looked into his eyes, like I had in our earlier days together, the yearning we had for one another was so strong that it took disciplined restraint for us both to keep our distance. When the night ended, we both hugged and said how glad we were to find one another again. We both agreed that we had needed the years to pass before we could really become just friends. Jim asked for my phone number and said we would keep in touch.

*

I had trouble sleeping that night when I got home. The adrenalin was pumping me up with excitement. I had never stopped loving Jim; even through the years with the editor I had never, ever given up that special space in my heart to anyone else, because it still belonged to Jim. A million thoughts ran through my head. Initially, there was the joy in seeing him again. As I relived the scenes of our tumultuous love affair, there were the warm and fuzzy moments, and also the pain of our breakup while still declaring our love for one another.

I reminisced about how many years it had really taken us to say good-bye. The friendship plan obviously hadn't worked for us back then because our emotions were still running high. We had both learned that we couldn't go from sharing a bed to shaking hands without feeling pain. Only distance could enable us to continue on with our lives. I wondered what was going to happen now, after so many years had passed. As much as I still loved him, I didn't think I could take any more heartache with him. Besides, I had never broken my promise to myself that I was done with married men, even if that rule had been made upon the end of *our* relationship.

A few days later, Jim called me. We spoke for a while, and, before hanging up, he asked me if I'd have dinner with him on the coming Saturday. I eagerly accepted. We went for Japanese food, my favorite, and were asked if we wanted to be seated at the teppanyaki table, where they cook right in front of you. Those tables had no privacy, as you were seated amongst another dozen people at the usually U-shaped tables. Jim graciously declined, and we sat in a nice cozy corner, drinking wine and catching up on our lives.

The electricity between us was humming all evening. It seemed every topic of conversation we had reverted back to our past. When I told Jim about the years I had endured in a toxic relationship, it angered him terribly. When I asked him how many relationships he'd had since ours, as I knew his virility would never keep him monogamous, he looked up at me with that all-familiar sadness in his beautiful, green eyes and said, "P.J., there was never another relationship after you. I've never stopped loving you." At that moment, I felt the arrow pierce my heart yet again. I could feel a tear slowly trace its way down my cheek. He had come out and said what I had known without a spoken word.

I believed him, because we had both bored holes in one another's hearts. I also believed he'd had no other relationships, for I knew well that his heart had been scarred by me and that this was the very reason we'd ended our romance. I began to remember that night way back when, on my couch in my first apartment, when he asked me if it had occurred to me that he might be falling in love with me. After all, that night was the beginning of our end. He had seemed frightened by the power of love that had overtaken him, because his policy had been to never stay with the same woman too long so as to avoid emotional involvement. He had broken his own rule with me, and that had been more than enough for him to never break that rule again.

After we finished dinner, Jim drove me home. I invited him to come up for a nightcap. When he walked inside my condo, he complimented my home, as it was a huge step up from my old apartment at Roseview. I poured us both a glass of wine, lit some candles, and turned on some Luther Vandross in the background. We cozied up together on the couch. We talked and drank some more wine, well into the wee hours of the night. Although Jim had told me that he still loved me and the night couldn't have been more romantic, there seemed to be an invisible shield between us, most definitely made of titanium, because it seemed to be the only thing stopping our mutual magnetic attraction from manifesting.

It was as though we were Adam and Eve and we had both taken a bite from the apple. In unspoken words, we both knew that if we ended up in the bedroom, we were walking right back into the past and might never get out again. I couldn't even imagine what was going through Jim's mind, because mine was in ten different directions. I was weighing a decade of wanting this man and wondering whether one night of rekindled passion would satisfy my longing for him or ruin the rest of my life by creating more heartache.

Eventually, our passions could no longer be contained.

There was no more conversation that could keep us from doing what we had both wanted to do since the evening began. Jim reached out and pulled me to him in a desperate embrace, and we held each other tight. Our eyes locked, and our lips followed. I thought I might burst with the passion inside me. Our kissing was almost violent with passion. Suddenly, when kissing was no longer enough for us, Jim stood up. He brushed the crease out of his pants and took my hand, standing me up and holding my face. A tear fell from his eye as he kissed me again, softly, and said it was time for him to go. He had openly admitted what I had been thinking, as though he had crept inside my head and read my thoughts. He told me how easy it would be for us to end up making love, and doing so would put us back where we had left off long ago. The hurt would be reignited, and the fact remained that he was still married and he still didn't want to tie up my life. Jim told me again that he would always love me and that we would always be friends. He told me that if I ever needed anything, he would be there for me.

I did need him. I needed him to fill the empty space in my heart with the piece that he had unknowingly been holding for so many years. But I never told him that. I admired his strength in leaving the way he did, because I surely would never have been able to deny him. Every few years, I ran into Jim. We became faraway friends, as it was just easier that way. When I last saw him about six years ago, a quarter of a century had passed since the first time we met, and I could still see the emptiness in his sad, beautiful, green eyes.

Catching My Breath

After I became single again, I felt as though God had given me a second life as a reward for having made such a bad mistake but then taking responsibility for it, climbing out of a harmful relationship with patience and endurance. I had never realized the value of my freedom as much as I did the day I was once again free. I lay on my bed and took in deep breaths as though breathing was a whole new experience, and it felt great. I was looking forward to my new freedom and to not having to answer to anyone. Things would be the way they used to be before I became a passive, quiet shadow of my former self.

I had learned many costly lessons in that toxic relationship. I had thought I could fix someone who was broken on my own, without the expertise of a professional. I realized that I had foolishly set low standards for myself, thinking that just because I had invested so much time in that relationship, I had an obligation to make it work. I was also foolish to believe that just because I was in my early thirties, I had to settle for a relationship as a natural part of growing up. I had felt that I invested too many years in that relationship and that starting over would be too long a climb.

That day, I stepped outside myself and took a really hard look at what had gone wrong. Hindsight is always clearest, and

I shook my head when I looked back on all the warning signs I hadn't paid any heed to, the things that should have made me flee. I made a mental list of some of those signs: I had put up with constantly being spoken to in a condescending manner, accompanied by a pointed index finger. I had given up the only home I had ever known to move in with a guy who never ceased to remind me that his home was *his* home. I had lived with a man whose temper could go off at any given moment, causing me to live like a nervous wreck. It had taken me way too long to realize I was living with an alcoholic, and I should have run like hell the first time he pushed me into a wall, a good indicator that I would someday have my life threatened by that man.

I spent a lot of time re-evaluating my life. Perhaps if I had acknowledged what I kept sweeping under the carpet during those years, my life would have gone in a different direction. I could only chalk things up as life lessons, because they certainly were. What hadn't killed me had certainly made me stronger and wiser, and I vowed to never make those same costly mistakes again, to never let my feelings or opinions stay shelved in fear. The next time around, I would learn to speak up. If I couldn't voice an opinion freely, without violence ensuing, I would be gone in a flash. I promised myself never to take shit from anyone again.

I thought I had wasted seven of the best years of my life but, as an eternal optimist, I tried to find the positive in everything. I had learned who I really was and realized what I would not tolerate in life. As the next few years passed, I found another reason to say that those years hadn't been wasted. I wondered if it had been God's plan for me to live and learn from that relationship until the time was right for me to meet the man who would become my husband.

Mother

As the years passed, my mother remained a sporadic presence in my life. I honestly never even thought much of it other than realizing I had found peace. I was quite content because, quite frankly, I had never felt very comfortable when she was around. When she was out of my life, I didn't have to listen to her theatrics and bullshit, but when I was in her presence, the old feelings of fear and discomfort would surge through me, leaving me with a knotted feeling in my stomach. She wasn't the sort of mother who would call to say hello or ask how I was feeling, only to complain about something or someone. Her complaints usually pertained to my siblings, and she would often call one of them to rant about me as well. I don't know if she had deluded herself into thinking she had an ally in any one of us, but my mother somehow didn't grasp that my siblings and I would compare notes on our varied conversations.

It seemed as though my mother's pedestal was crumbling as the years went by. Physically, she was still very beautiful—ageless, it seemed. Her face was still lineless and firm, and she still had her fiery, red hair well into her mid fifties. If I could have inherited one thing from her, I would have wanted to keep my good skin through aging! By that time, not only had my siblings and I caught on to her manipulative, conniving ways, but most others who knew her were also aware.

After she came back from Florida, she worked intermittently at both my brothers' businesses. Without going into great detail, I'll say that this only lasted a few years. No matter what my mother did or where she went, she still needed the spotlight on her. It was like a sickness. I had spent over thirty years without my mother really being part of my life, but she had suddenly appeared back in our midst, acting as though the past had never happened and we had to listen to her, jump for her, and most of all, struggle through the guilt trips she constantly dished out. She had resumed her feelings of entitlement as a mother, though she had essentially become a stranger to me, a stranger who had some kind of invisible grip on my conscience.

I had always tried to keep the peace between my siblings if there were arguments. I just didn't like living in discord, and perhaps that was why I had always kept my mouth shut when my mother would go off on a tangent. I had been raised to never talk back to my elders, and even though my mother was hardly around, I didn't dare open my mouth to her when she was. I just couldn't seem to take being yelled at or threatened with guilt, or maybe I didn't want to provoke a slap in the face, so I remained voiceless around my mother.

For years I had put up with my mother's bad-mouthing of others, either in person or by phone, and I would let her rant without uttering a word in response. She wasn't even looking for acknowledgment—she just wanted someone to listen to her venting. I cringed any time I would see her number displayed on my phone, automatically feeling those familiar knots in my stomach. It was equally unsettling for me to have to call her, and it seemed as though our phone conversations were all one-sided. Occasionally, if I didn't comment on what she was saying, she would scream at me shrilly, "Are you listening to me?" I would say yes, and she would continue on with her rant.

It was never simple with her. Anything she spoke of had to be dramatized for effect. By that time in her life, even the men who used to swarm around her were slowly disappearing. Nobody wanted to be around negativity, and men in particular weren't interested in being bossed around and yelled at. It was as though my mother's mighty empire was crumbling. My father was no longer around for her to extract money from, and her boyfriends had all but vanished, so it seemed she had come home to roost and expected her children to be her obedient little soldiers, standing at attention for her command.

She still had the gambling addiction, only the days of the racetrack had passed and the new flavor had become bingo and casinos. My brothers had donated a lot to her cause, but that gravy train came to an end after a few years. It was difficult being her daughter, never feeling at ease around her and trying to conceal it all my life. I never felt I hated her, but as the years passed, I grew to resent her. I felt deprived of a real mother. I had spent my childhood missing her, but I found myself grateful that she hadn't been around in the years that followed. When she came back into my life, it was only to complicate it.

When I was younger, I used to hope she would try to make amends for the past and apologize, and I might have been open to giving her a chance back in my young adult years. Unfortunately, that never happened, because she didn't seem to think there was a problem and she therefore had nothing to apologize for. So my resentment grew, as I couldn't get past wondering what gave her the right to come barging back into my life when it suited her only to use me as a sounding board or add her two cents. It was frustrating not being able to have one interesting conversation as mother and daughter. I also couldn't get over how a mother could phone her daughter and never ask about her or how she was. How did she still have this power over her children? We had feared and been forced to respect our mother since childhood, and though I had always wished I had the nerve to tell her how I felt, I never dared. She couldn't handle the truth about herself, and that was why she had lived in denial for so long.

As I got older, I truly began to pity her. I had studied her for years, as I had to find some sense of how this woman had come to be while still trying my best not to be confronted by her. I wanted to justify her actions. I didn't need to agree with them or accept them, but I wanted to understand why she acted the way she did. I had often wished I could tell her just what I thought it was that had made her into such a cool, calculating woman, but I never could. The years had cautioned me, and I knew better. She lived so deeply in denial that the only place that conversation could have taken me was back to my fear of her response.

I just couldn't peg what it was that made me so afraid of her—her raging temper, her hurtful words, her continual guilt trips? She would never own up to anything I could tell her, even if I tried to speak with kindness. She would often retort, "You think you're so goddamn smart. You think you know everything." Her famous line was, "I'm your mother, young lady, and don't you forget it," as though that statement resolved everything. Nobody ever got away with voicing an opinion that didn't reflect her greatness without receiving a razor-sharp comment in return. It was just easier to swallow my words to her as time went by, much easier than having my insides shaken and stirred.

I really believe that somewhere in her denial, she knew I had her number, and she resented me for it. I allowed my mother to verbally thrash me for years because in a secret, melancholy way, I had begun to realize why she was who she was. I never condoned or accepted her actions, but I knew how they had snowballed throughout her life and left her with a giant ego. I had the map of my mother's life all drawn up: Her mother had died young, leaving her to fend for herself at a young age. I didn't know much about her childhood, as nobody ever talked much about it, but the tidbits I had received from Aunty Sherry told me that their own mother had been a beautiful, vivacious woman who loved to party, and I knew my grandfather had loved going to the racetrack.

I could see where those traits fit in. I knew my mother had visions of a good life, and her strongest assets were her looks, undoubtedly inherited from her own mother. She met my dad, though to this day I don't believe she truly loved him. She intentionally got pregnant by my father so he would marry her, and she established herself as his wife. My father was so enamored by her that he gave up all control and power to her, and she used this to her full advantage. She'd had no guidance in her life to even know what it meant to be a good wife or mother, and she was so hungry for material things that she would go to any lengths to attain them.

She was also so starved for attention that the affections of my father were not enough for her, so she used her beauty, her pretentious charms, and my dad's money to earn her social status. She needed to be the center of attention. Her things always had to be better than someone else's. What she spoke had to be truth, even when it wasn't, and any story she told had to be exaggerated or dramatized to prompt praise and compliments. She had a desperate need to feel important, and her life was like a fantasy she had dreamt up from childhood and brought to fruition through her ego. She was the director, and nobody would ever be able to take her power.

I could see right through her. The strange part was that I believed she had built her ego as a defense mechanism against her own insecurities. If she could appear to be the best, tell the biggest tales, and scream and rant to maintain her power, then she wouldn't have to acknowledge to herself who she really was. Yes, I knew her well. As she became older, the players in her life slowly vanished after years of enduring her sharp-tongued tantrums, and I watched her anger escalate as she strived to hold on to what she had worked so hard all her life to attain.

Finding the Future

It had been a month since I was newly single, and I was treasuring my newly acquired freedom.

One night, after I had finished closing up a blackjack game at work, I decided it wasn't too late to pop in and say hi to my friend Terri, who was working just across the street in another hall. Those events usually ran until about 1:00 AM, and it was only 11:30. As I walked through the very crowded room, the man from whom I had recently bought my car approached me. I remember feeling caught very off guard, as I liked to keep my private life private. I didn't like casual acquaintances in my life to know how I made my living. It wasn't that I was ashamed; it was more of a privacy issue with me. Some people got the wrong impression, and I didn't feel I should have to justify my job.

His name was Lou. He gave me a hug and asked me what I was doing there, and I politely explained that I had just closed up and wanted to visit with Terri. Lou had another gentleman in tow, who appeared to be a good ten to fifteen years older. Lou introduced this man to me as his father-in-law, Gordon. We shook hands and chatted for a few minutes, and then I said, "It was nice seeing you, Lou. Now you know my secret life." We both chuckled, and I bid Gordon good-bye as I went to look for Terri.

I had the same policy about dating men I met at stag parties as I had at bars when I was younger: I never went out with them. I think this stemmed from my inner need to be appreciated for who I was and not just for my looks. I didn't want to feel as though I had been asked out because someone was under the influence of alcohol or because I seemed like an easy mark. I had spent my life building my reputation as a kind, intelligent, compassionate, fun-loving spirit, and I took pride in the fact that nobody could say I was easy to take advantage of. Being attractive and working amongst men, I found myself getting approached constantly. With my flaming-red hair and my matching personality, there never seemed to be a lack of attention, though I never took this for granted.

I was proud of who I had become, and knew I had worked hard to get there. I strived to be the best person I could be, inside and out. Perhaps because of my mother issues, I wanted to be accepted for all of me and not just for my looks. I had a knack for being friendly and charismatic, but I still knew how to keep my invisible guard up. I thoroughly enjoyed my profession: I loved the social interaction, dealing cards, and working independently. I knew how to make good tips, and they were the bread and butter of my paycheck. Although I was sometimes still insecure with myself, I never let it show outwardly. I always came off as confident and wore a smile. Those attributes helped me earn a good living.

Two days after meeting Lou at the banquet hall, he called me. He said he hoped I didn't mind him taking my phone number out of his file and calling, but Gordon had apparently been quite attracted to me and had asked Lou for my number, but Lou wouldn't give it to him without my permission. Apparently, Lou and Gordon worked together at the car dealership. I was flattered, but I told Lou I wasn't interested in going out with anyone at that point, as I was still celebrating my independence. I was also concerned that Gordon was quite a bit older than I was, even though he didn't look his age. This information didn't seem to deter Gordon, though! He called me only minutes later, and we talked for a good while. Near the end of our conversation, I thanked him for calling and repeated what I had previously told Lou: I just wasn't interested in dating anyone. He seemed to understand, and I didn't hear back from him again until December of that same year, eight months later.

I had stuck to my plan of no dating, and I was enjoying life. I was also working a lot, and December was a particularly busy time for functions, with the Christmas season approaching. Gordon called me again, this time offering a gig, as he was organizing a stag party and needed a card dealer. I was impressed that he had kept my number but never harassed me about going out, and I really wanted to work that stag, especially since the location was so close to where I lived. He hadn't given me much notice, though, and I was already booked that same night for a charity function. I told him this and presented him with a counter offer. I knew the charity function was a short stint and that I could be finished there around 10:00 PM, so I asked him if he wouldn't mind holding off on the card game until around 10:30. The deal was done.

*

When I got to the stag party, I set up the table and charged Gordon a nominal fee before informing him that I was to keep all my tips. That didn't seem to faze him, as I sensed he was grateful to have me there. Gordon seemed like a very sweet person, a perfect gentleman. He had blackish hair with streaks of silver, with a well-trimmed beard and narrow mustache, both grey. He had warm, blue eyes, and he wasn't too tall. I guessed him to be around five-foot seven, but everyone was taller than me, so height had never really been an issue. His frame was strong, and he carried a bit of a paunch, which I supposed was the result of a good life. He actually struck me as being a cuddly teddy bear, and he looked a great deal like Kenny Rogers, the singer.

Gordon never left the blackjack table. As the night drew to a close, it seemed he didn't want to leave. We had talked a lot that evening and had actually developed quite a rapport. He had also tipped me ridiculously, too much for what the short stint warranted. I told him I couldn't keep all the tips, because it just wasn't right that I had made more money than the groom, but Gordon insisted I keep what I earned. I ended up keeping a reasonable amount and giving him back the rest, and after I packed up and was ready to leave, Gordon asked me if I wanted to go for a coffee with him. I politely refused and told him it was late—he'd had enough to drink and should go home. He wasn't obnoxiously drunk, but it *was* late, and I wanted to end the night on a respectable note. I told Gordon I thought he was a true gentleman and that I had really enjoyed his company, so I would love to have coffee with him another time.

Another time turned out to be the next day. Gordon called me the next morning and asked me to meet him later that afternoon. We met and talked for a few hours, and we had a lot in common. We both found it strange that we had never met before, because our paths had crossed many times. It seemed that back in my nightclub days, he and I had frequented the same clubs. What really fascinated me was that Gordon had kept a condo in my building, two floors above mine, for two years while I was living there. We found it odd that we had never encountered one another while living in the same building, but I supposed there was a reason for everything. If we had met in the past, the timing wouldn't have been right for us, and divine intervention thus kept me tied up until the time was right. We made plans to go for dinner and dancing later that week.

I sensed there were already sparks developing between us, but my past experience had definitely toughened up my persona. I had vowed I would never let anyone shit on me again or take advantage of me, and I had promised myself that the next guy in my life had to have all the proper prerequisites to pass the gentleman test: He had to have a good demeanor, a pleasant personality, and most of all, a good sense of humor. I wanted to laugh, because that was the person I was, and I had let all my joy be taken once before. I was never again going to be with someone who could burst my balloon. I wanted to remain free to be myself and not conform to be what somebody else wanted me to be. Most importantly, I wasn't going to stay quiet when I felt the need to express myself. I had become a very determined person with a strong personality, and only a strong man who could stand up to me would ever have a chance of winning my heart.

Friday came, and Gordon and I were to go out on our first real date. I thought it might not happen, because there had been a terrible snowstorm that day. I lived in the northern part of Toronto, and Gordon worked only ten minutes away from me although he lived downtown. I remember thinking it wasn't a good idea for us to be driving in the storm—in fact, it was crazy. Gordon would pick me up and take us downtown, and then he would have to drive me back up north and drive back downtown to go home, which I thought was absurd. I didn't think anyone would want to trek around town with such inclement weather, but it didn't stop Gordon. He was downstairs waiting eagerly for me to get in the car so we could head out, and his tenacity was one of the first things I admired about him.

We had a great time talking the night away. Gordon was very charming and still behaving like a perfect gentleman. When it was time to leave, it felt as though the long drive home passed too quickly. We never seemed to be at a loss for words. As much as I enjoyed myself, I still prepared a mental test for Gordon. I wanted to believe his sincerity, and I told myself that when he dropped me off, he would not be invited upstairs, and if he got pushy about it, there would be no more dates. I also hoped he wouldn't try to get all passionate when kissing me good night, as that would count as a strike against him as well.

When we finally arrived in front of my building, Gordon put the car in park. He took my hand and leaned over, kissing me gently and quickly on the lips. He told me he would call me the next day, and I was elated. He had passed the first test!

We went on a few more dates, and the attraction between us became quite mutual, though I still kept my guard up. I continually felt the need to express to Gordon that I was not about to take any shit from a man and that I would never allow myself to be tied down by anyone, but I found Gordon to be a fun-loving man who knew how to treat a woman. By no means was he as talkative as me, so he let me speak and paid attention to everything I had to say. I admired him for never fleeing from all my speeches about what I was and wasn't going to tolerate from a man anymore. That was definitely a part of his character that aided my attraction to him. I knew that my strong personality had intimidated some men in the past, but Gordon's determination to have me never faltered through any tough words I dished out. He admired my strength, and I also thought it amused him.

After one week of dating, Gordon announced with a big grin on his face that he was going to marry me one day. I laughed at what I thought was a ridiculous statement, telling him I was never getting married, as I had decided quite young and had managed to stick to the plan. It did puzzle me to hear him say this, because he had been divorced for some years and it seemed that he was quite a lady's man. Despite all my words, I knew at that time, deep in my soul, that it was quite possible he might be right. Our connection was so uncanny. I knew he was crazy about me, and I suspected he might possibly be the man I could marry, even though the thought of marriage really scared me. At the time, I was already praying that he wouldn't spring the "I love you" on me, because I certainly wasn't ready for those words.

On our third date, Gordon confessed that he wasn't living alone. I got very angry with him and told him I couldn't deal with lies. He begged me to listen and reminded me that he had never lied; he had simply omitted this tiny tidbit of information. I gave him my speech about how I didn't go out with married men—or, in his case, involved men—and had given up that heartache years ago. I asked him why he hadn't told me from the beginning of our relationship, and his answer was pure and simple. He said, "I knew that if I told you, you wouldn't go out with me, so please let me explain."

"What is there to explain?" I asked.

He proceeded to fill me in on the circumstances of his living conditions. Apparently, he had shared a condo with a woman for the past five years, and, though the relationship had fizzled out about two years back, they had reached an agreement to stay together in their respective bedrooms, both doing their own thing. This didn't sit right with me, but I actually believed him. Somehow, I knew he had told me the truth.

Gordon and I began seeing one another almost every day. He worked close by my home, and this afforded us opportunities to see more of each other. He would come by for lunch or dinner or even just for coffee, and we really enjoyed spending time together.

We were only into our third week of dating when those scary words seemed to come out of his mouth. I had sensed it but was hoping I wouldn't hear him say the words, as I wasn't ready to hear them and certainly wasn't ready to reciprocate. I loved the way he gently held my face and looked into my eyes when he'd kiss me, and I had no doubt there was magic between us, but I was still feeling a bit raw from my recent ordeal. I remember the moment when Gordon told me he loved me. I sensed the words about to spill from his lips, and I quickly put my finger up to them as if to silence him. He said it anyway. I gave him a hug and chuckled, telling him I couldn't hear those words just yet. He responded, "I can wait, but I can't help but tell you, so for now I'll say *I like you.*" I had to laugh. He was just so cute, and he had such a way with words.

I knew my feelings had grown immensely for Gordon in the short time we had been together. This was something that concerned me, because it had been many years since I had felt so loved and comfortable with a man. I felt as though it was all happening so fast, and I didn't want to make any more mistakes with men. I wanted things to progress slowly so that I could gauge my true feelings.

Within six weeks of dating, Gordon took me to Las Vegas. He knew how much I loved the old charm the city had, even though its landscape was growing more like a metropolis as the years passed. I had already been there a few times, and I loved the excitement of just being there. The weather was so nice and dry, the shopping was great, and I loved to play cards, even though I was a very conservative gambler. I was sure the years of witnessing my mother's addictive gambling habits had played some part in that, and I was happy to see that Gordon had the same theory: Never lose more than you can afford. We both allotted ourselves a set amount of money per day, and if that was gone, there were plenty of other things to do. I loved the respect Gordon had for money, because I'd always had a secret fear about ending up with a man who might throw caution to the wind. I could never live comfortably worrying about the future—I needed stability in my life, having come from such instability.

A few months into our relationship, I was undoubtedly falling in love with Gordon. He continued telling me, "I like you," on a constant basis, and he always smiled devilishly when he said it. I knew very well those were his substitute words for the real thing, which I had forbidden him to say. By that time, I knew him well and trusted the sincerity of his feelings for me. I found it so freeing to be able to act completely natural around him. I wasn't ever afraid of him, nor was I afraid that my occasional outbursts on a bad day would scare him away. We were solid, and for the first time in my life, I felt as though I could say whatever I was feeling. We didn't have to play games or skirt around issues.

One weekend in March of 1997, barely four months after we started dating, Gordon took me away to a lovely inn up in cottage country. It was a very cold, snowy weekend, and it seemed the further we drove north, the colder it became. We had a lovely room with a fireplace, overlooking the mountains and ski trails. It was very romantic. This inn was a complex of three buildings, and the dining hall was two buildings over, a short five-minute walk, but we still had to layer up with coats and boots, as it was a bit of a trudge with the snow and the wind.

The next morning, when I woke up, Gordon wasn't in the room. Five minutes later, I heard heavy banging against the door. I quickly ran over and asked who was there, and Gordon responded with, "Could you please open the door?" Quizzically, I opened it to find a true Kodak moment. Gordon was standing there, fully garbed in his winter gear, holding a large tray with covered plates and a big thermos of coffee. I was completely awestruck. He told me that he wanted to surprise me with breakfast in bed. Something in that moment touched me to the very core of my heart, and that was when I knew I loved him completely. That was also the day I discovered that my heart had truly become whole again, and I freely gave Gordon the newly acquired piece that had been missing for so many years.

As I cupped his frozen face in my hands and kissed him sweetly, he hugged me tight. He looked into my eyes and reaffirmed, "I like you." It was then that I told him I loved him, and he asked me if that meant he was allowed to say it now, too. We looked at one another and burst out laughing, the same way we still do today.

As the months passed, Gordon was busy devising a plan

to move out of his current living arrangement. He was a very clever man, and when his inner wheels were in motion, he didn't always share his thinking until his plans came to fruition. This was a habit of his that drove me crazy, because I was the type of person who needed to know things immediately. I had nicknamed him my man on a mission, because when Gordon set his mind to something, he always made it happen. Nonetheless, I helped him pack up his condo and move out. By November of that same year, we were living together in my condo. Gordon had also invested in a little townhome up north, backing onto the water, where he could park his beloved boat. We spent many weekends up there as we enjoyed our happy life together.

*

Gordon and I moved to a bigger condo within the same building only six months after he moved in with me. At the close of 1998, on New Year's Eve, Gordon proposed to me with an exquisite diamond ring, and I found my future. I had stopped working casinos and private functions, not out of jealousy on Gordon's part but because he didn't want me driving alone late at night. I had always worked, and it felt strange for me not to be making my own money. I did eventually end up going to work part time, managing an office for a building company.

In that new year of 1999, I began making our wedding plans. I really didn't want a big wedding, as I couldn't visualize myself ever walking down an aisle without my father there to give me away. I asked Gordon if we could just go to Las Vegas and get married there, just the two of us. After all, I was pretty much on the fence as to whether I wanted to include my mother in my wedding as anything more than a guest, because she was barely in my life any longer. As for Gordon's family, I think they were still struggling to accept me in their lives. I could understand that, though, because his daughters were all close in age to me. They wanted to protect their father, as I had mine, so I had yet to earn my wings. I'm sure they wanted to know for sure that I loved their father and that I was going to stay for the duration.

Gordon's vote won out. He was truly a traditionalist, and he didn't feel it was right for me not to have a traditional wedding experience, because I had never before been married. Months into my planning of the wedding, the question still plagued me as to who would walk me down the aisle. I had proudly bought my wedding gown by myself and had arranged the whole wedding. During those same months, Gordon wanted us to buy a house. We would often go for drives, looking around, and eventually we found a lovely street where homes were just being built in Richmond Hill. We decided to customize a home there, and we sold our condo and our place up north to build that house.

It was a very busy year between running up north, packing up the condo, and planning the wedding. We were to move into our new home three days after our wedding, which was to be in October, on Thanksgiving weekend. One day I got a call from my mother, who had yet to even see my current home, let alone know about how busy I was packing two homes and constantly checking on the construction of a third. It never even fazed me that she had shown no interest nor partaken in any of my wedding preparations. Neither had she offered to come with me to see my gown. The last time I had seen her was just after I got engaged, when I had gone over to my sister's house on New Year's Day to show her my ring and my mother happened to come by.

It was early September, and I was in my last stages of fittings on my wedding gown. My mother asked me if she could come along with me for my fitting so she could see it, and I was actually taken aback at this request. I honestly didn't know if I was more shocked at her request or if I was once again feeling sorry for her that she hadn't been part of my wedding preparations.

For some strange reason, the guilt that I felt from my mother had never subsided, even when she wasn't in my life. Instead of being angry at her for not showing any interest in my life, I had been carrying guilt at not including her in my plans, as though this had been a wrongdoing on my part. This seemed to be the way I let my guilt guide me. I always felt bad for her without stopping and thinking about how bizarre it was that a mother wouldn't want to share in her first child's wedding. How truly sad it was that I had become so used to living my life without her that it never even bothered me not to have her with me through it all.

I felt compelled not to shut her out, so I took her with me for a final fitting. After the fitting, I don't know why, but I couldn't overcome the sadness I felt for her. It was as though all the empty years between us were staring me in the face. I silently recalled monumental moments in my life that she was never there for, and I remembered the many awful things she had said and done to me in the past. I relived how she had ripped my father's heart to pieces, and I remembered the countless times she had instilled fear into the very core of my existence, yet I looked at her with true pity. I was looking at a woman who had commanded the world around her and broken many hearts along the way, a woman who had manipulated her way through life, and when there was nobody left to take her verbal thrashings, she turned them on her children.

She was in her late fifties now, but her face still retained its former beauty, still without a line. Her posture was no longer erect, and she walked considerably slower. She'd also had a stent placed near her heart, as her arteries were quite clogged at that point, probably from her years of hard living and smoking over a pack of cigarettes a day. Her empire had clearly fallen, and in that moment, in all my realization, I felt as though I should once more reach out. I offered her the honor of walking me down the aisle.

She eagerly accepted.

Married and Sick

Time flew by as though there weren't enough hours in the day. My wedding day came and went and, only days after, we moved into our new home. I was exhausted; the past six months had caught up with me all at once, it seemed. I wasn't really feeling too well, and my stomach had been giving me trouble off and on for weeks at that point, but I didn't have time to be sick, so I became good friends with Zantac.

However, I was finding that my issues were now becoming more than a match for Zantac. As I unpacked box after box, I became weaker and found myself spending more and more time in the bathroom. By the time a week had passed, I was going to the bathroom about twenty-five times a day and couldn't eat. The temperature outside was a balmy seventy degrees, quite unseasonably warm for October, but I spent the days lying on the floor, wrapped in a blanket in front of the fireplace. My husband called me several times a day to check up on me, as he was worried sick. He came home early for several days and continually found me on the floor, shivering in front of that same fireplace. He begged me to let him take me to a doctor, but I wouldn't go, as my determination to fight the weakness and the pain was fueled by the humiliating thought of being in transit to the doctor and having to go to the bathroom.

Into the second week of enduring the pain in my upper

stomach it became intolerable. This had now become more than an issue of exhaustion. One night while lying in bed, I felt as though I could no longer live through the pain. I began to scream out to my husband, "Please kill me! Just get a knife and end this for me." I had reached the end of my tolerance—it seemed that nothing mattered anymore and that dying would be a welcome relief.

The ambulance arrived quickly. When I was finally injected with morphine, it was the strangest feeling. The pain was no longer prominent, but it felt like it had only been masked. I could still feel the stabbing pains as a dull ache, locked away at a distance. During my morphine-induced weeks, I was put through dozens of tests, yet the doctors couldn't find what was wrong with me. At the time, they were thinking it was some sort of cancer. Between feeling awful and my drug-induced sleeping off and on through those days, I was too sick to even worry about what was wrong with me. Finally, the last horrible test revealed what was wrong with me: I was diagnosed with Crohn's disease.

I didn't know much about the disease, but I had experienced enough to know it had the propensity to be life threatening. However, I remember my husband being overjoyed, thanking God and crying happily when he found out I wasn't dying of cancer. After the doctor gave me the basics of the disease and put me on several prescriptions, I was sent home after spending three weeks in the hospital. My doctor did tell me that those drugs weren't 100 percent foolproof, and he explained how the disease attacks the intestines, causing painful inflammation. He told me that if the pills didn't contain the flare-up, I would have to go on steroids.

The word *steroid* was very scary for me. All I knew about them was that they left terrible side effects, the most concerning of which was that they made you fat. Ever since I stopped being a chubby teenager, I had made it my life's mission to never be fat again, and the thought of steroids scared me more than the damn disease. I had been home for just short of three weeks, and I didn't seem to be getting any better. Once again, the ambulance took me back to the hospital. After experimenting with several other drugs during the next few weeks, there seemed to be no more alternatives than to be put on steroids. I was told I would be taking them for approximately three months and that I would then gradually be weaned off them.

It was a horrible time. Those drugs wouldn't allow me to sleep and blew me up like an inflatable doll. Within only three weeks, I had gained twenty pounds. I shuddered at the thought of having to go outside the house. I was grateful it was winter and that if I absolutely had to go out, I could wrap a long scarf around my neck and head, almost covering them. My face looked stretched out like a saucer, something like the reflection you see if you look into a round stainless steel kettle, stretched and distorted. My vanity had suffered, and I was sick and weak.

About two months into my steroid voyage, I was finding it difficult to walk and had taken a few spills down the stairs. It was at this time that I made a decision. I had to take matters into my own hands, because I could see the big picture as to where things were heading. I had to become proactive and learn about my own body and health. At the time, all I knew was that the steroids and other medications were weakening my bones. I was told I would need those meds the rest of my life, and I had visions of living in a wheelchair. I was determined that this wasn't going to happen to me.

I suppose it was still my nature to be a curious person, needing the answers for everything. I had always tried to help others, but the time had come to help myself. I needed to start researching my disease and looking at alternative medicine, because clearly there was no cure for this disease, and the drugs to keep me in remission were having devastating side effects. I was new to the world of computers, so Gordon bought me one. In the interim of learning how to use it by reading *Windows for*

Dummies, I sent Gordon to Chapters, my local bookstore, to buy me numerous books on the disease.

It turned out that my doctor hadn't given me all the information about Crohn's. I learned that it was an autoimmune disease and that the steroids were leaching calcium from my bones at an alarming rate, as would the medication I was to continue on after the steroids. I also found something very interesting, something the doctor had also never told me: Certain foods, particularly dairy and wheat, exacerbate this disease. That was enough for me to take action. I made a list of the supplements I was going to put myself on, and I sent my husband to go buy them for me. At that point in time, I still had about a month left on the steroids, and I continued to finish them off while I began my new regimen with the supplements. I also started my new diet.

Two months had passed since I was off steroids, and I was actually feeling great for the first time in well over six months. The new diet was difficult to adapt to at first, but it helped me live pain free, and that was worth giving up any food. I had also regained my strength. It was once again great to be alive. The only thing left for me to do was get off the lifelong meds I had been prescribed, as I was sure my new alternative medicine and diet were what had given me my newfound strength. All I wanted was to be drug-free and well.

I called my gastroenterologist and told him I would like to go through the horrible test again, the one that had shown the ulcerated state of my intestines. At the time, I had been told that the state of my intestines would never improve, and the goal was to not allow them to get worse. I told him how good I had been feeling and about what I had been doing to attain my good state of health. I just knew that something in my body had changed for the good. He didn't refuse me, but he didn't really see the point of putting me through the test again, as he felt the end result would be the same.

What a victorious feeling I had when I went back to my

doctor to discuss the test results! He showed me the X-rays taken of my intestines when I was first diagnosed and compared them with my recent results. I will never forget that day. My doctor said, "If you weren't my patient when you were so sick, I would never have believed these X-rays belonged to the same person." He then pronounced me free from the need for all my meds. Those words were music to my ears. I felt like God had spared me and given me a second lease on life.

The thing I found odd about the conversation with the doctor was that when I asked him whether he wanted to know what I was taking and doing to make myself better, he responded, "Whatever you're doing, keep it up." I thought, *Wow, what a blow*. His statement only fueled my interest in alternative medicine and opened my eyes wide about the medical system. I made it my business to learn about holistic health, because I was living it.

There's still a stigma attached to alternative medicine, but nowhere near that of fourteen years ago. Back then, Western medical professionals didn't acknowledge or really understand how things worked. Now, naturopathy has gained a whole new respect, and even the pharmacies have taken a piece of the action by supplying supplements. I started researching natural healthcare and subscribing to wellness magazines, and I found myself a truly amazing naturopath a few years after I began my healing. He has given me an excellent quality of life.

There is still no cure for Crohn's disease, but there are many changes one can make to achieve a high quality of life. We all make choices, and since that time, I never experienced that pain or suffering again. My lifestyle change allowed me to live like a normal person, almost forgetting I have a disease. I have endured a few flare-ups through the years with no pain, mostly just fatigue and loss of appetite, along with having to live near a bathroom for a week or so. If a flare-up didn't calm down after a week, I would go see my naturopath, who would put me on an intravenous cocktail for about two hours. By the time I'd leave, I was better.

Life was good, and I was almost back to my old busy self again. The only lingering terrible side effect I still had to conquer was the thirty-five steroidal pounds that took almost two stubborn years to get rid of. This wasn't for a lack of proper diet or exercise—according to the doctor, hormonal weight gain takes a lot longer to get rid of, as steroids wreak havoc on hormones, producing lots of cortisol that forms into fat. However, my determination and perseverance finally won out.

As I began my journey into naturopathic health, it seemed to me that not only Western doctors but my own family didn't understand how it worked. When I'd eagerly speak of all I was learning and how great I was feeling as a living testament to it, they seemed to fluff it off as if it were some hocus-pocus regimen. I really didn't care, as I was over the moon, and so was my husband. We believed.

This was a time of rediscovering life for me. I was learning about how the human body worked and reading a lot about emotional happiness, really broadening my mind with self-help books. My husband trusted me with all my discoveries, and he had no qualms about following along with everything I suggested he take to maintain good health. My friends were urging me to become a licensed nutritionist or something of the like, but I didn't want to get that far into it, as I wanted to learn for my own purposes. This never stopped friends from phoning me when they had minor issues and asking me for a recommendation for something they could take to alleviate their problems, though. Ironically, whenever I tried to suggest something helpful to my family, they wouldn't be interested. I knew I wasn't about to change the world, but at least I was willing to help.

I no longer bothered suggesting anything to family members if they were ill, because I wasn't interested in being ridiculed. I realized I couldn't save everybody. I supposed it was true what people said about going through a life-altering situation: It really makes one see things from another perspective. Knowing that my father had died young with heart issues, and watching my mother follow the same path with her heart troubles, I had become determined not to end up like them. I tried to offer my mother healthy advice and proposed some beneficial supplements she should be taking, but that just proved to be a waste of time. Certainly, if she had a stent already and still hadn't quit smoking, I wasn't going to make much of a difference. I never even received any thanks for my concern—I was instead made to feel as though I was some kind of annoying door-to-door salesman. Nothing had changed with my mother. She was only growing more and more bitter and sarcastic. The few times I did see her, she would stir up that old knotted feeling in my stomach with her knifed tongue.

By now, I felt I had to call her once in a while out of obligation, but I dreaded calling her more with every number I dialed. I didn't know how I had become caught in that web of obligation after so many years of her absence. It was as though my siblings and I had been programmed since childhood to jump for her, almost as though we were her possessions. The odd thing was that we all allowed it, though I think I allowed it because I continually felt sorry for her. My siblings and I would bitch about my mother and compare tales of her imagined stories, how she would bad-mouth any one of us to another. We continued to let her spew, and none of us stood up to her to shut her up. The invisible power she held over us continued.

Marriage and Mother

I had been married for about two years. After I had gotten my illness under control, life was good. It seemed the only stressors in my life came from my mother's harrowing phone calls. Never, ever did I receive a call just to say hello. There always seemed to be an agenda. By this time, my mother wasn't well, as she had heart issues. I did worry for her, but unfortunately I never got the opportunity to express any compassion, because her sarcasm and denigration of others seemed to hamper any good intentions I had. She only called to vent her anger at the world. It seemed nobody could do right by her. If I tried to change the subject and talk about a happy incident regarding me or my husband, she would shoot back with something like, "Of course you care more about your husband than you do me." She knew how to churn my insides. She could never seem to be happy for anyone, as her life wasn't what she wanted it to be.

My husband could see the angst she caused me and used to mime at me to hang up the phone, but I just couldn't. I let her use me as a sounding board for years, and as much as she gave me grief, I felt sorry for her. My sister had more guts than I did. Melanie would sometimes talk back to my mother or just hang up on her, managing not to speak to her for months on end, but somehow they always reconciled. My sister always spoke her mind with no fear of guilt, and I often wished I had her gumption. Melanie didn't pity my mother the way I did, and I think most of those reconciliations were for the sake of her children. She urged me several times through the years to learn how to just hang up on my mother and stop taking the shit she repeatedly doled out to me, but I never seemed to have the heart to do it.

Later that year, my mother needed to have open-heart surgery, a triple bypass. My siblings and I all took turns taking her to doctors, and we were all there at the hospital during her surgery. We didn't talk much during the long waiting hours. It seemed as though we were all lost in ourselves, perhaps taking stock of the events we had experienced with our mother. I know I was. After her hospital stay, she was to go to a rehabilitation facility for a few weeks, and then she would need additional care for another month at home, except she lived alone.

While she was in rehab, we all did our best to visit her daily or at least take turns, allowing each of us a day off. We would bring her food, and I would take her laundry, wash it, and bring it back to her. It seemed that whatever we did was never enough for her. She was just plain miserable to be around, and she complained about everything and everyone. I just couldn't seem to do right by her. My mother would tell me I didn't stay long enough, I didn't bring the right food, and the list would go on. I always tried to cheer her up. Once I told her it was a beautiful day outside and she should be grateful to be alive, but how I wanted to retract those words as soon as they left my lips. I got a verbal thrashing: What the hell should she be grateful for? Her life sucked, nobody cared about her, blah, blah, blah. I knew I was never going to win no matter how nice I tried to be.

When the time came for her release, the doctor said she had to have someone stay with her for a few weeks. Internally, I gasped. That was a punishment I didn't want to be part of. I also thought how truly sad it was that at a time when a mother needed her children, it was so difficult for us to be around her, happy to help. Fear rushed through me that I would be the one chosen to look after her, and anxiety about living in close proximity to her negativity for so long began to gnaw away at my insides.

My brothers made it quite clear that they weren't going to take her in and subject their wives to a toxic environment. My sister was a single mother with three children, and at the time she had three dogs. I was the one with the big house, with no kids, and I was no longer working, so I won the honor of taking my mother in while she convalesced.

My stomach was doing cartwheels at the thought of living in close quarters with my mother. I hadn't lived under the same roof with her for over a quarter of a century, and even then, she had barely been home. I hadn't had much contact with her through the years, either, and now that she was sick, it would become my duty to look after her. I had no idea how I was going to break this news to my husband. I knew he would never deny me, but I also knew he most certainly wasn't going to be happy with the imposition on our lifestyle or the toll it was going to take on me emotionally.

I brought my mother to my home. She had her own guest-room and washroom. I was a clean freak, and so was she, so I knew all would be well in that department. I was also a good cook, as I'd had decades of experience, having cooked for my family since I was eleven. She reigned over the TV in the family room, as my husband happily retired to the basement to watch his sports and find solace every night. He worked hard at being gracious to my mother, although he inwardly couldn't wait for us to regain our private life. The situation was very awkward, as I had never spent this much time with my mother and was uncomfortable around her. We locked horns plenty, as was to be expected. She had way too much access to me, and the experience was a long way from a mother–daughter reunion. I made sure she was looked after, but I took any opportunity I could to get out of the house.

One day, she had an argument with my sister on the phone and carried it on with me when my sister eventually hung up on her. When I wouldn't agree with her, her wrath once again turned to me. At that point, about three weeks into her stay with me, she informed me that she'd had enough of all of us and was going home, and she carried on martyring herself about how she didn't need any of us and was going to take a cab. I'd had enough aggravation by then, as I could do no right by her and was glad she was leaving, but still, I couldn't let her take a cab. I felt guilty yet again that I would be a terrible daughter if I didn't drive her home. I also didn't want to give her the chance to use it against me that I had *made* her take a cab, a tale I was sure she would talk about down the road, how I threw her out in a taxi. I insisted on packing her things and taking her home. I knew in my soul that was what she wanted anyway, but she wouldn't be happy unless she could make me feel bad, and she knew well that of all of her children, she could always rely on my compassion to get me to succumb to her whims.

I found the whole experience with her so sad and pathetic. Her kids couldn't be allowed to feel compassion for her because she always managed to find a way to kill those feelings with her outbursts. She loved to play the victim. I had struggled with my mother issues all my life, letting her demean me and hurt my feelings over and over. She had a unique way of making me feel inadequate, and I really didn't even think that it was done purposely; it was just her nature. She took full advantage of my temperament because I let her, and I realized as I got older that it wasn't worth it to disagree with her stories. I let her rant, whereas my siblings had learned to simply hang up the phone. I didn't want to hurt her feelings, so I constantly put mine aside, but it didn't matter. I was never going to win with her.

After she recovered from her surgery, my mother resumed her life with even more bitterness. She went back to playing bingo and casino slots. This was an obsession for her; this was her life. My brothers indulged her financially to try to make her happy, *try* being the operative word. It just seemed that nothing was ever good enough. She was falling deeper and deeper into an abyss of misery. I knew she hated what her life had become, and any friends she had left were disappearing one by one. She had managed to push away everyone with her sarcasm and bitterness. Nobody wanted to hear it anymore.

A couple of years had passed since my mother's surgery. She was getting weaker and suffering residual effects, including shortness of breath and trouble with her legs. She could no longer drive, and she was relying more on us kids to do her errands and take her to doctors' appointments. This put me in more contact with her than I cared to have. Nothing any of us did for her was appreciated or went without comment. It was also difficult spending time around her because there was nothing to talk about. My mother wasn't interested in hearing anything good that may have been happening in our lives, because her life sucked. We had to always watch our words around her, because she would use them back on us, twisted out of context.

She couldn't tolerate hearing anything nice without a seething comment, and she was so jealous of any happiness we shared with our spouses' families that she felt compelled to make comparisons and ask why she wasn't part of those happy occasions. The funny part was that through all her guilt trips, we had all invited her to many gatherings only to see her take pleasure in declining and then throwing it back in our faces. My mother just didn't want any part of the joy in our lives. Instead, she chose to bad-mouth people. This was how she found fulfillment. It was very sad to look at her and see what she had become, and I was even sadder that she couldn't be grateful for whatever she did have left in her life. She was so full of anger, yet she didn't even realize it.

One day, my mother bit the hand that fed her, complaining to Rory after he told her he would no longer contribute to her gambling habit. Yes, she was no longer driving, but that didn't mean her and her oxygen tank couldn't go to the casino by bus. She said some terrible things to Rory that struck him deeply in his heart, and that was the last my mother ever saw or heard from him. That left only three of us to share the responsibilities. As my mother's health deteriorated, she became mostly confined to her little apartment. She relied on us for groceries and to take her to her doctors' visits. Those were pretty much the only times she got out. Robby was paying someone to look after her a few days a week, and he took her to most of her appointments. My sister had been through quite a few arguments with my mother by this time, but she always came back to share in the responsibilities. Melanie and I took turns taking my mother her groceries and visiting her. It was grueling and unsettling.

One day, my mother used her sharp tongue on my sister for the last time. Melanie answered her with a spewing vengeance. It was as though my sister was releasing everything she had kept pent up inside for years. Melanie clicked off the phone and never spoke to my mother again. That left only me and Robby with the responsibilities. My mother had only two children left in her life.

I became the sole grocery shopper, and I always made sure my mother had enough food for the week, because going to see her once a week was more than my nerves could handle. She would make me a list, and every week I prayed that none of the items on the list would be out of stock, because I would never hear the end of it. I would be told I was too busy thinking about myself, or that if I had gone the day before I would have found everything on the list. If I had to buy apples, they had to be just the right size, or I was going to hear about it. I could never just drop off the groceries and leave or I would have to endure a speech about how I had no time for her. Once I stayed and watched a movie with my mother, and after staying almost four agonizing hours with her, there was no gratitude. Instead she said, "What? You stayed for half an hour and you think you did me a fucking favor?" Those were the conversations I had to look forward to.

I realized at that point in my life that I had tried for so many years to please her to no avail. I believed she resented her life and that when she looked at me, I represented her past, everything she still wanted to be. I sensed a certain jealousy of me, since I had grown to somewhat resemble her looks as I aged. I think that, for her, it was like looking in a mirror at what she once had been. Sadly, she was not only losing her looks, but she had no inner goodness to compensate for the lost physical attributes. She just refused to share anybody's joy because she hated her own life.

The pressure of being the only daughter was mounting inside me. Her phone calls came more often than I could digest, as her bitterness increased through time. I was listening to trash talk about Rory and Melanie constantly, because my mother had been banished from their lives. My stomach still churned when I answered her calls, and that didn't help the disease I was living with, especially since stress could so easily set me off in a flare-up. My husband begged me to walk away from the toxicity I constantly endured, as the guilt was eating me alive, guilt I had carried all my life. I was torn. I couldn't stand being around my mother, yet I didn't have the heart to abandon her. Somehow I always felt it was my obligation to try to do the right thing by her because she had given birth to me. I felt I owed her. I worried about her health, and every time I visualized her living alone, with nobody in her life, it tugged at my heart. It was a vicious pattern of continually going back for more when I knew very well that the results would be the same.

I tried to get her to agree to take some alternative medicine, as she constantly complained about how sick she was. She would laugh at me sarcastically, telling me that hocus-pocus shit wasn't for her. She knocked every idea I had. My sister had long begged me to throw in the towel with my mother, as she couldn't understand the hold my mother had on me. Truth be told, I didn't know myself why I felt so compelled to stick around, aside from the fact that my mother was an older sick person and she was alone.

To everyone who knew her, it was quite evident why she was alone. The guilt trips had been deeply rooted inside me since childhood. I had feared her back then, and I supposed that feeling never really went away. I wanted peace and harmony. I wanted to make everything right so my mother would have no reason to bestow her wrath on me. I had just never learned that her actions were beyond my control.

Hearts Afire

nother year passed, and my husband and I had moved again into the new home we had built. I was busy decorating our lovely new house while I still diligently carried out my duties to my mother. Needless to say, between the stressors of my mother and moving, my Crohn's disease had become quite active on and off throughout that year. I somehow managed to keep my disease in a controllable state: no pain, just becoming best friends with the bathroom.

About a year later, I had noticed this tiny, red, shiny dot on my right forearm. I probably wouldn't have paid it any mind other than the fact that it never seemed to go away. My curiosity, as always, kept me wondering why it was there. It was really no bigger than the size of a pinhead, and most people wouldn't have paid it any mind. For months I'd occasionally glance at it and wonder why it was there. It didn't bother me or itch—it was just there. I looked at it for months before my curiosity got the better of me. I had previously shown it to my husband's old dermatologist, and he had said it was nothing, but I believe everything has a reason, and if I weren't that kind of person, well, I wouldn't be here now, writing this book.

I decided I wanted a second opinion. I found a new dermatologist in August of 2005, and I was able to get an appointment in January 2006. When I went to the appointment, as fate had chosen my corner, the doctor I had booked was absent and I was sent in to see his associate, Dr. Allen. She was a lovely, soft-spoken woman in her early forties. We seemed to forge an instant rapport, especially since I gave her the backstory on how inquisitively I had been following this insignificant spot and how proactive I was with my health. She looked at it and said that it was probably nothing, but she wanted to be cautious and snip it off for analysis. I was happy to find that she took me seriously enough to have a closer look. Dr. Allen told me to come back in two weeks for the results, and I told her that would work out great, as my husband and I were about to leave for a two-week winter vacation to Mexico.

When I went back to see Dr. Allen for my results, still basking in the afterglow of my beautiful trip, she informed me that the results had come back negative. It was nothing. Just as I was breathing a sigh of relief, she added, "Although the result is negative, I would like to send you to have a painless test done." I remember looking at her quizzically, head on, into her big brown eyes.

"What?" I said. She told me that this type of spot could sometimes show up in relation to an underlying heart issue, and I looked at her in disbelief. I asked her if she was kidding, knowing very well that a doctor doesn't joke about such matters. She reiterated that the test was just a precaution and that she only wanted to rule it out.

A week later I was hooked up to wires and laden with gel as the lab technician, Len, scanned my heart. The procedure was an echo Doppler, and it was painless save for the cold gel and the equally cold ultrasonic wand Len was streaming around my chest. The test was to last about an hour, and in that time, Len and I became fast friends. We chatted about everything under the sun as I watched my heart beat on the screen beside me. About an hour into the scan, Len's conversation seemed to come to an abrupt halt. I glanced up at the screen and noticed a strange sight. It seemed that with every breath I took, a tiny, tonsil-like ball suspended from my heart flicked up and down. I didn't hesitate to ask Len what I was looking at.

Len sat silently for a moment. He reached up to scratch his head as though in disbelief, and then he rolled his swivel chair back away from the screen. He then looked at me in mortification and informed me that he was going to call in the cardiologist. In an instant, I replied, "Cut the shit, Len. What the hell am I looking at?"

Diagnosis: a myxomatous fibroma tumor suspended from my mitral valve. This was a very rare tumor, seldom diagnosed until autopsy due to its symptomless presence. I was in shock to the very depths of my being. My world had been rocked. I couldn't speak or shed a tear. I couldn't remember driving home after feeling I had been given a death sentence. My first thought was that I couldn't call my husband at work with such devastating news—I couldn't even find the words I'd use to tell him when he did get home.

I looked at the call display as my phone rang shortly after I got home and saw Gordon's number. As the tears splashed down my face, I let the phone ring until the machine picked it up. It was better to let him think it was a typical day. Usually when I went out, I made an afternoon of it. Within an hour of my getting home, Dr. Allen called me. She was the first person I spoke with since I had gotten home and planted myself in a chair, still in shock. She greeted me with apologies, as she had just received my results back from the echo test. Dr. Allen was kind and empathetic. I could tell she felt awful that her sending me for the test had made her the bearer of this frightening situation. I sensed her compassion and told her she had potentially saved my life. I cried out my fears and questions to her as I began to feel an incredible bond with this angel of mercy. That was how I regarded her from that day forward.

Dr. Allen told me she would send me to one of the best heart surgeons in Toronto, who specialized in those types of tumors. I had put my faith in her and her generous offering before I even went to my regular doctor. When we hung up, the first phone call I made was to my naturopath, Dr. Eric. He had given me my quality of life, and we shared a patient–doctor friendship. Dr. Eric always had solutions, and at that point in time, I needed his words of wisdom. He gave me an outline of what was going to ensue, and he promised he would do everything to make my healing easier. Dr. Eric asked me to come see him the next morning so we could just talk. He knew the state of mind I was in, and he knew I needed his reassurance. Dr. Eric spent almost two hours with me, just talking. He told me there was no alternative to having the surgery—it had to be done to remove the life-threatening tumor, but he promised to work closely with me through the ordeal, and he did.

Suffice it to say, breaking this news to my husband was one of the hardest things I'd ever done. My poor husband had suffered so much grief already with my prior illness, and he was very reliant on my strength of character to always pull us out if something bad happened. I was his rock, and now something bad was happening to me. I had hoped to get all my crying out of my system before he got home from work so that I could remain stoic for him. I didn't want to fall apart. Gordon adored me, and I didn't want to deliver this blow to him. I couldn't help but cry, as I found there seemed to be an overabundant supply of tears, but I remained strong and promised him I wouldn't die. He needed to hear this even if neither of us was sure we could believe it. I kept a strong attitude around Gordon to keep him from falling apart at the thought of possibly losing me.

Within days, I was sitting in the office of Dr. Letterman, my soon-to-be heart surgeon. He explained the tumor, its location, the tests I would endure in the coming days to prepare me for the open-heart surgery, and finally the surgery itself. When Dr. Letterman questioned me as to how on earth this tumor had been detected and I told him about my journey of the little red dot, he was mystified as to how a dermatologist could even have suspected such a link from the dot to the heart. He also remarked how lucky I was that it had been detected. Apparently, I would have been dead within six months if it wasn't found. The tumor was loosely suspended from my valve, and within time it would eventually have fallen off and embolized in my lung. He told me I would have died instantly, most likely in my sleep.

*

It seemed to all happen so quickly. The time from my diagnosis to the surgery was about seven weeks. During that time of prayer and fear, I reassessed my life and found new appreciation for every breath I took. It wasn't that I didn't always appreciate my life, but, like most people, I'd often taken things for granted. I began reading about angels and trying to understand the way the universe worked. For some reason, I just knew it wasn't my time to go yet and that I would survive. I went over and over the journey of discovering the spot on my arm and all the divine intervention along the way that had led me to Dr. Allen and her uncanny discovery of the tumor. I just refused to believe anything other than that I was meant to live because of the way it had all come about. Those were the thoughts that kept me sane through the fear. I kept positive thoughts the whole time and trained my mind not to go to the dark side, not even for a single moment. I learned a lot about the laws of attraction, and the motto I lived by was, "You get what you focus on," so I focused on healing before the surgery.

My husband walked around in silence, in deep thought, unable to talk about the what-ifs. His fear ran deeper than mine, so I cornered him one day, feeling I needed to give him a pep talk. I told him I knew of his unspoken fears, and I tried to make him understand the importance of positive thinking and the laws of attraction. I explained to him that positivity was like a power prayer, and his focus on the good would help me win my battle. He hugged me so tightly, as though I was the last remaining hand that could have reached out to save him from falling off a cliff, and then he cried. I had only seen my husband cry once since I had known him. I held his face and looked him straight in the eye, and I said to him, "I am not going to die, do you hear me?" It was like a great weight had been lifted off him as the sun shone. He did believe.

The weeks prior to my surgery, I went to see my mother once. I was busy going for lots of tests and spending time with those in my life who gave me joy. However, it was peaceful with my mother during those weeks, because she didn't give me any grief when she called.

When the day of my surgery approached, my fears came to the surface and I became overwhelmed. Up until that point, I had been keeping a positive outlook. My spiritual readings had gotten me through the fear and taught me to visualize myself healthy and alive. It took lots of mental discipline not to allow myself to go to the dark side, but I was so well versed by then on the power of my focus that the fear of delving into the possibility of a negative outcome was not even an option.

The thing that spooked me the most was that I was not checked into the hospital the day before surgery, nor was I given any type of a sedative. My surgery was set for seven in the morning on Wednesday, April 26, and I was to just show up, having showered with antibacterial soap, at five. All I could think of while showering at three in the morning was the unimaginable inevitability of having my chest sawn open in four hours. There were moments when I actually thought I was going to have a heart attack from the overwhelming fear before I even got there.

My husband and my sister were with me. I had previously made a pact with my sister that there were to be no tears, and this was working fine until the time came for the nurse to wheel me on the gurney to the operating room. My sister leaned over to hug me as I joked around in nervousness, and her tears were welling up. I reminded her of our pact, with tears in my own eyes, and told her I would see her soon. Then my husband came to me and quickly kissed me before darting off in haste. One might expect my husband's kiss good-bye to be a lot more intense, but I knew my husband very well. He was so distraught that if he even uttered one word, he would have fallen apart. No words were necessary. I watched him catch up to my sister, and I saw them embrace one another, sharing their tears.

As the nurse wheeled me inside the operating room, I was definitely feeling too alert. I observed a team of nurses counting instruments, the bright lights, and then I cast my eyes on the heart–lung machine. I had been fully informed on how that baby was going to sustain my life while Dr. Letterman held my heart in his hands to repair me. I was moved onto the operating table. By then I knew I had seen too much. By my side was a compassionate man, the anesthesiologist, and I asked him to please put me out immediately, as the fear was becoming almost too much for me to bear. He kindly asked me to count backwards from ten . . . but I didn't even remember nine.

I first woke up around midnight. Apparently, I had been in a drug-induced sleep while my body came out of hypothermia. When I opened my eyes, I was in a very dark and silent intensive care unit, and I sensed what felt like an angel over my shoulder. The angel turned out to be a nurse waiting for me to wake up. My throat was parched, and my lips felt as though they had been glued together. In a barely audible voice, I asked for water. The nurse informed me that my system was not yet ready for drinking, but she kindly brought me some ice chips and gently brought them to my mouth, tenderly rubbing them along my lips with her gloved hand. Five days later, I went home.

*

I was grateful for everything in my life—I was grateful just to be alive. I was blessed to have had such a wonderful heart surgeon. I had joked around with him in the days before my surgery, asking him if he could please keep my incision neat and inconspicuous with his tailored expertise. I didn't want a zipper. He had laughed at my vanity and promised he would do it himself, and now most people don't even notice my ten-inch scar.

My naturopath, Dr. Eric, sped my healing along with his remedies and came to my home to visit me a few times, and my sister left her teenage kids for three weeks to move in with me and help my husband take care of me. She showered me and constantly propped me up so I would be comfortable. The bed-time ritual was a difficult one, as I had to sleep sitting up for almost two months, but my sister had the system down pat, with an organized method of how to place the pillows around me nightly so I could sleep in the upright position. My husband was so grateful to have my sister with me so he could feel at peace when he went to work and know that I was being cared for. Gordon would reward Melanie by bringing home "good food," as they liked to joke.

My sister often teased me for being a health nut, as she was quite the opposite. I kept nothing in my kitchen that interested her, certainly nothing with wheat or dairy. Gordon was secretly glad to have Melanie around so they could indulge together in the foods I never even let him eat. Melanie and I were complete polar opposites, but when it came down to the crunch, she was always there for me. I would laugh in the mornings when she made her comical digs while craving a cup of tea with milk and some *real* toast, as she called it. She would then take herself over to Tim Horton's, where she could satisfy her taste buds, though she never bothered going to buy herself a loaf of bread or a carton of milk!

I was also fortunate to have my good friends, who not only came to visit but all chipped in with housework. My two oldest best friends, Zan and Bri, had always been a mainstay in my life. Although Zan was living in England, that didn't stop her from coming to see me. As well, my good friend Tonie lived across the street and would come over often to offer meals or bring groceries and vacuum for me. I was truly blessed to have such a wonderful circle of friends. By the end of July, I began to feel like myself again. I had gained a whole new respect for those who underwent heart surgery. It was a scary event, and a very hard and long recovery. Although I wasn't permitted to lift anything for six months, I began to resume life as I had known it.

Going into the following year, I again resumed my responsibilities with my mother. It seemed that, as time passed, our tumultuous relationship went back to normal. The niceties she had put forth during my illness seemed to disappear. I was once again back to the same old antics with her. I wasn't sure whether perhaps Dr. Letterman had cleaned out all the toxic buildup of guilt in my heart while he was repairing it, or whether it was divine intervention, but I had reached a point where the mountain of shit I had taken from my mother over a lifetime was ready to topple over. After experiencing a life-altering situation, I took a good, hard look at my life. Anyone who knew me well knew that the relationship I had with my mother was consuming me internally. I just wanted her to be well and leave me alone. I didn't want to be around the negativity, and I wanted so badly to tell her this just once in my life. I wanted to scream out my feelings.

Guilt

It wasn't long before my tank finally hit empty, sapping the last ounce of my tolerance. The event may have been trivial, but for me, it was the last time I would allow myself to be a verbal punching bag. I had been doing my duty, putting in the time, trying to do right by my mother, but I had reached a point where I just couldn't take her venom any longer.

I tried my best to take her out to bingo once in a while, as that was one of my mother's few pleasures, though I didn't have the funds to go often, or the time, or even the inclination. My mother failed to understand that I had a life and wasn't available for her every whim. She didn't respect my time, nor did she appreciate the effort it took me just to take her out. Bingo may have only been a two-hour session, but it cost me almost the whole day to take her, plus a taxing effect on my nervous system. By the time I'd driven to pick her up, gotten her and her walker and oxygen apparatus loaded up, and gotten her to the bingo hall early enough for her to pick her seat, plus the same to get her home, it had taken up the better part of the day. A decade past, I had enjoyed playing bingo with friends, before life had become so busy and the price to play became ridiculously expensive.

One day, I received a call from my mother. She began the conversation with the daily grind before gradually getting to the point of her call, the accusation. Apparently, somebody who knew somebody she knew had told my mother they had seen me at bingo. This was unacceptable to her. At first I remained silent, although my mind was swirling with the words my sister had so often said to me: "Just hang up already! How many more years do you need to subject yourself to her shit?"

I replied, "I haven't been to bingo since I last took you."

Suddenly, with a demonically shrill voice and a devious chuckle, she said, "Don't lie to me! I know you were there."

I repeated to her that I hadn't been there. As I found myself defending the truth, I also wondered what the hell I was defending myself for. I was angry—I shouldn't have had to report to her where and when I was going anywhere, but most of all, I hadn't even gone to bingo, and she was calling me a liar.

She called me a liar one more time before I snapped. It was as though forty-eight years had suddenly broken down my invisible shield, which could no longer protect me. My body began to shake uncontrollably, and a voice from within me lashed out in a pitch I hadn't even known I was capable of producing. I screamed, "I am *not* a liar! I refuse to take your toxicity anymore! You've pushed everyone out of your life. You're never happy unless you can make somebody miserable, because you can't stand to see anybody happy or successful. I feel sorry for you! A woman in your state should be thankful for the children you do have, but now you've lost three. Don't ever call this number again!"

This was the first time in my life that I had ever raised my voice to her. Years of pent-up resentment had spilled from my soul, and I banged the phone down so hard I thought I had broken it. I stood in my living room in shock, still shaking and hyperventilating from the wrath I had just spewed.

When I caught my breath and finished sobbing, I called my sister to inform her about what had just transpired. She commended me for finally letting go, but she also added that she knew me well and told me that I would carry the guilt for what I had done. My sister felt no remorse for her decision. I then called Robby to sadly inform him that he was the last man standing. I apologized to him for leaving him alone to bear the load by himself, but I told him that I had been eaten alive for way too many years. Robby knew what I had endured, what we had all endured with my mother, but he knew she pressed special buttons with me because I allowed it. Robby told me he understood why I had to do it, but this left him in a very dissatisfying position. Robby had taken his lumps from my mother, but up until that time she had tried to hold her tongue more with him than she had with the rest of us.

In the next few years, my relationship with Robby seemed to become strained. Robby didn't often say what he was feeling, so I had to read between the lines to understand his thoughts. I didn't have to be a mind-reader to sense that Robby resented being saddled with our mother and the responsibilities. He got a taste of what it was like to have her demands constantly in his life, and, with time, my mother no longer even held her tongue-lashings back from Robby, as he was the only one left for her to vent to.

I felt terrible leaving my mother to Robby, but I had to save myself. Robby had always put in his time, but my mother had been so much easier on him when she had my sister and me around to abuse. Robby had now gotten a rotten sampling of what Melanie and I had endured for years. I had apologized to Robby many times for leaving him in the lurch, but somehow I felt like my words couldn't compensate for his load. Toxicity has a way of pulling a family apart.

Although it was freeing to break the chains that bound me to my mother's grip, not a day has gone by that I don't think of her without feeling sorrow and pity for her. Guilt is like a stubborn stain, very hard to erase. I still battle my inner struggles as I seek to find peace with my resolution. The day I snapped and found my voice, confronting my mother, was very cathartic, but it didn't fully free me of guilt. It took me a long time and many decades of life to figure out that I couldn't fix everything or everyone myself. Sometimes, one just has to learn to walk away.

*

Six years have gone by since the day I last spoke to my mother. My life is full, but the guilt still lingers within me. Although I have banished her from my life and I no longer have to endure her constant badgering and verbal thrashings, I still struggle with the guilt that plagues me on a daily basis. Somehow, my heart doesn't feel free of her. I still pray for my mother, and even with this distance between us, the guilt I carry for leaving never seems to diminish. I have learned to forgive her silently, within my own heart. No matter what mixed emotions roll through my subconscious, I cannot go back.

One would think that after all the years of taunting and belittling me, my mother would have mellowed as she got older and sicker. Perhaps she could have seen her mistakes and apologized with what little time she has left on this earth. But the years seemed to fuel her anger at life even more, and she still questions what she has done wrong and why her children don't speak to her.

Before our final falling out, I had gone back to her on a previous occasion after not talking to her for almost a year. I had received a call from a family friend, begging me to go see my mother, who was in the hospital at that time. That person informed me that my mother might be dying, and the guilt was once again laid upon me. I was terrified of seeing my mother, but the guilt got the best of me. Robby agreed to meet me at the entrance of the hospital so he could go in with me as my protector, as he had so often been. I was so nervous about what to expect, about how I would be received.

She appeared happy to see me, and not much was said for

about five minutes. Then my mother began telling me her point of view on our last disagreement. I politely told her that I hadn't come to rehash our arguments and that I wasn't going to get involved again, so she promised to let it go. However, when Robby went back to work and I was left alone with my mother, it was just like old times. She began ranting at me, and I allowed it. I was sucked back into her vortex. Even when she thought she might be dying, she just couldn't help herself. I was once again delusional, thinking that maybe she would have been happy to see me again and would have wanted to make amends. I thought she might be glad to have yet another chance to realize what she had lost. However, with such precious time left in the world, that somehow just wasn't important to her.

That experience, along with those that came before, has convinced me to maintain my distance. I still struggle with the thoughts I have of my mother. She's alone now, living on borrowed days. Still, after half a century, I fear being in her presence. The constant memories of how she treated me don't seem to dissipate. I feel so conflicted, because I don't miss her, yet I feel sorry for her as a human being. I feel sorry for her as a mother. She is probably feeling abandoned without even realizing that she abandoned us long ago.

I am left with my tattered emotions regarding my mother. From what I hear about her, the bitterness has not subsided. While I pray for her and worry from a distance, I have steeled myself to the decision not to go back. I sometimes try to anticipate what I will feel when she is gone, to try to find some peace with myself, but nobody can really predict the reactions of the human heart.

My Beloved Husband

Positivity is a strange animal. Let it loose, and it roams as far as anyone will allow it.

My husband has always been my balancing stone, and I his rock. Four years after my heart surgery, he was diagnosed with stage four prostate cancer. Once again, my world was rocked. I learned that when life keeps throwing curveballs at you, you just have to learn to catch.

When we received the devastating news that he had cancer, at first I cried, and then I put on my big-girl pants. Between waiting for tests and starting radiation there were a few months, and with everything I had learned about that ugly monster cancer, I didn't want to waste any time. We headed straight to Dr. Eric, who put Gordon on a supplemental regimen to build up his immune system. He also set him up on weekly intravenous cocktails of high doses of vitamin C. Dr. Eric runs an extensive clinic of alternative and complementary medicine for cancer patients as part of his practice, and high doses of vitamin C are known to kill off cancer cells. However, this must be taken intravenously, as the high dosages cannot be ingested.

This gave us hope and peace of mind that we were being proactive in fighting this disease while waiting for radiation therapy to begin. Doing nothing while we waited would have just given those bastard cancer cells a chance to grow, and we were doing everything in our power to halt the process. My husband was a healthy seventy-one-year-old man when he was diagnosed, and we both truly believed that because of the healthy lifestyle I had implemented and the ongoing guidance of Dr. Eric through the years, we would conquer the beast.

The intravenous cocktails gave Gordon renewed vigor and strength even as the radiation ravaged his insides, sucking all his energy. Gordon was a trooper, my hero. He stoically plodded on as he took the radiation five days a week for two months straight. Day after day he would trudge out very early in the morning down to Sunnybrook Hospital so that he could get treated early and then continue on to work. At first Lou or I drove him, but after about two weeks, Gordon insisted that he was fine to go on his own. I worried incessantly about him, but he was adamant about it, and I recognized that he needed to assert his independence. He was a very proud man and wanted to maintain a sense of normalcy in his routine. He was a brave soldier. The actual radiation didn't hurt him while it was being performed, but the residual damage gave him problems. The treatments made him very tired, and I worried about him driving home from work, barely able to keep his eyes open. He came home early in those times and slept many hours.

This man, my husband, would never surrender to defeat. We were so thankful to Dr. Eric because he had prescribed some amazing cream to alleviate the stinging burn on Gordon's pelvic region from repeated radiation on the same area for two months. During this period and the two-year follow-up, Gordon was also given a biannual injection to suppress circulating testosterone from instigating cancer growth for this type of hormonal cancer.

When Gordon completed his radiation therapy, I witnessed how the process had taken its toll on him. I saw his once strong arms become flaccid, and his shoulders and frame seemed to narrow, but his spirit never did. His bowels and rectum were severely ravaged from the constant burning action against the nearby prostate gland, but he overcame all that as well over time. Dr. Eric had put Gordon on remedies to strengthen the bowels and suppositories to alleviate the burn. Gordon also underwent two minor rectal surgeries to cauterize some collapsed blood vessels, which had caused profuse rectal bleeding. Those were quite trying times, but we got through it one day at a time.

Perseverance is a funny thing. If you don't give up and don't lose your spirit through adversity, you can summon up the courage to keep plowing on. Now, three years later, my husband is cancer-free.

Epilogue

Only with age do we realize how quickly the years pass. The minutes turn to hours, and suddenly there are never enough of them in a day to accomplish all we set out to do. When we're young, we can't wait to grow up and do grown-up things, because we're ignorant to the real responsibilities that come along with age. The young and innocent can only imagine the freedoms they will be afforded when they're older, though they don't realize the many sacrifices that must be made along the way to enable us to attain such freedoms.

I have become very involved with reading about and practicing spirituality. Between my illness and trying to figure out how to live peacefully with my overwhelming mother issues, I became a ferocious reader over the years. My reading got me through many somber moments in life, and I also began to take my writing more seriously. Journaling became an important friend to me, and the urge to write this book began stirring within.

Somehow, we all seem to find a way to muddle through life, each event forming the people we become. We choose what to do with our acquired knowledge: We can climb the peaks and prevail, or we can become submerged in the abyssal depths of our conflicts. Many of us form character by rising up from adversity. I love my life and choose to live it with no regrets. I have battled tattered emotions and illness and have constantly struggled with my past. Growing up on a wing and a prayer sometimes led me to make bad decisions, but I have learned from them and will continue to learn. As long as we are living and breathing and doing, we are learning.

Life has so much to offer us, sometimes even in mysterious ways. We all have the choice to make the most of our lives and conquer the challenges life puts forth to us. My curiosity keeps me in constant search of satisfactory answers, and my determination to succeed in any venture drives me to follow through until I reach a positive resolution.

This is who I am.

Don't forget to be frivolous and to frolic, to feel sexy, to be kind. Remember your passions and act on them. Smile like the world is filming you. Stand tall as a peacock, proud of what you believe in. Strut your feathers. Love yourself. Treat others as you wish to be treated . . . and don't forget to breathe.

End

About the Author

D.G. Kaye was born and resides in Toronto, Canada. She loves to read, shop, travel, and play poker when she gets the chance.

Kaye has been writing about her thoughts on life since she was a young girl, as pen and paper became her emotional outlet. Through the years of compiling her thoughts and memories in a journal, she wrote this book as a cathartic release. Kaye wanted to share her story in recognition of the many people who struggle with their past, perhaps shedding light on how powerfully a mother can impact a child throughout her life.

This is Kaye's debut book. She is currently working on her second book, a humorous satire on menopause, which will be released in spring/summer of 2014.

Visit her website and blog at www.dgkayewriter.com.
Follow on Twitter www.twitter.com/pokercubster
Follow on Facebook www.facebook.com/dgkaye
If you would like to contact D.G. or sign up for upcoming updates to her next book, email her at
d.g.kaye.writer@gmail.com or join her mailing list at her website www.dgkayewriter.com

Printed in Great Britain
by Amazon